To the Cross and Beyond
Cycle A Sermons for Lent and Easter

*Based on the Gospel Readings of the
Revised Common Lectionary*

David O. Bales

CSS Publishing Co., Inc.
Lima, Ohio

FIRST EDITION
Copyright © 2010
by CSS Publishing Co., Inc.

Library of Congress Cataloging-in-Publication Data
Bales, David O., 1948-
    To the cross and beyond : and other Cycle A sermons for Lent, Easter ; based on the gospel readings of the Revised common lectionary / David O. Bales. -- 1st ed.
    ISBN 0-7880-2634-8 (alk. paper)
    1. Lent--Sermons. 2. Lenten sermons. 3. Jesus Christ--Passion--Sermons. 4. Easter--Sermons. 5. Bible. N.T. Gospels--Sermons. 6. Church year sermons. 7. Common lectionary (1992) I. Title.

BV85.B325 2010
252'.62--dc22   2010040629

ISBN-13: 978-0-7880-2634-8
ISBN-10: 0-7880-2634-8   PRINTED IN USA

To the preachers:

Phil Moran

and James Aalgaard

With gratitude

Foreword

For ministers who have preached their way through the lectionary years A, B, and C, and begun the circuit again, there is a challenge, and a danger, and an opportunity. The challenge: What to do with a text you already covered a few years ago? The danger is that the answer to the challenge will be the same old thing, creating the conditions for a tired ministry and preaching imprisoned in shades of gray. Yet, there is also the opportunity to explore familiar territory with new eyes. For those who are tempted to redundancy, or whose pastoral responsibilities leave little time for renewed study and creative energy, or who seek the vitality aroused by an unusual, and unusually intelligent perspective, this collection of sermons by Reverend Dave Bales is a gift.

In a word, I would describe this collection of sermons as "Fresh." Fresh in terms of perspective, energy, language, and spiritual significance. In many ways, the sermon on Nicodemus serves well as a metaphor for this whole book. The old and venerable member of the Sanhedrin is tired, dry, "empty as a pond in a drought." Yet, his encounter with Jesus offers him a fresh glimpse of the possible, of a new kind of life, of what refilling that pond might mean. Nicodemus received the gift of a fresh start, and in its own humble way, this little book offers the gift of a fresh start, breathing a new life from above into the proclamation of the greatest of all stories.

Rev. Mark D. Smith, Ph.D.
Professor of History and
Vice President for Academic Affairs
The College of Idaho

Acknowledgments

I would like to thank the following congregations for inviting me to preach the sermons in this book. Grace to you and peace.

First Presbyterian Church, Emmett, Idaho
St. Paul Lutheran Church, Ontario, Oregon
Community Presbyterian Church, Pilot Rock, Oregon
Kingman Memorial Community Church, Adrian, Oregon
First Presbyterian Church of Homedale, Idaho
Peace Memorial Presbyterian Church, Klamath Falls, Oregon
Grace Lutheran Church, Vale, Oregon
Church of the Redeemer, Weiser, Idaho
Covenant Presbyterian Church, Boise, Idaho

Table of Contents

Ash Wednesday   9
Matthew 6:1-6, 16-21
The Right Reason

Lent 1   17
Matthew 4:1-11
Jesus Tempted in Us

Lent 2   25
John 3:1-17
Nicodemus: A Young Old Man

Lent 3   33
John 4:5-42
The Bridge at Sychar

Lent 4   41
John 9:1-41
Seeing Jesus

Lent 5   47
John 11:1-45
Where Is Jesus?

Passion / Palm Sunday   55
Matthew 26:14—27:66
Remembering Jesus

Maundy Thursday   63
John 13:1-17, 31b-35
Looking Down on God

Good Friday   **69**
John 18:1—19:42
Suffered under (Saint) Pontius Pilate

Easter Day   **77**
John 20:1-18
Putting the World Back Together

Easter 2   **85**
John 20:19-31
He's Back

Easter 3   **91**
Luke 24:13-35
On the Road with Jesus

Easter 4   **97**
John 10:1-10
The Door of the Cross

Easter 5   **105**
John 14:1-14
Praying in Jesus' Name

Easter 6   **113**
John 14:15-21
Duuuh!

Ascension of Our Lord   **121**
Luke 24:44-53
He Ascended into Heaven

Easter 7   **129**
John 17:1-11
Jesus' Prayer: The Pause in the Battle

Ash Wednesday
Matthew 6:1-6, 16-21

The Right Reason

Two mornings a week I drive from Ontario, Oregon, to Caldwell, Idaho, to teach at College of Idaho. When gas prices shot up I got into the habit of driving slowly and increasing my miles per gallon. Driving slowly isn't a hazard while in the country between the two towns. However, when I draw near Caldwell, the signs reduce speed to 65. There, in order to stay up with the larger flow of traffic, I must increase my speed so I don't jam up traffic. We all end up driving a safe speed, but we do so for different reasons.

Our Lord Jesus in Matthew 6 mentions three religious acts that are being performed for reasons that are "different" from what he approves. He talks about people who give alms, which means money for charity; yet, their doing so is theatrical, making their giving with a flourish and a bow, all so they'll be noticed and admired by others.

Jesus is upset over the reason they're doing it. A few sentences earlier in this same Sermon on the Mount Jesus commands his students, "let your light shine before others, so that they may see your good works and give glory to your Father in heaven" (Matthew 5:16). It's not wrong to do good things; it's why you're doing them.

Second, Jesus instructs in prayer not to be like the show-offs who stand to pray on the street corners in order to be seen. Jesus isn't against public prayer. He prayed publicly. It's the reason you do so. If your praying tempts you to dramatize your religion for the sake of others, go somewhere private to pray.

Finally, Jesus takes a swipe at the phonies who cosmetically publicize that they're fasting. Again, Jesus fasted for religious reasons but did so away from everyone.

It's not as though Jesus is just a religious contrarian who takes a stand against everything the way it is. The physicist J. Robert Oppenheimer was instrumental in creating the atom bombs dropped on Japan to end WWII. When he was in graduate school in Germany, his fellow students remember how irritating he was. He'd often interrupt people, even the professor, to step up to the blackboard, take the chalk, and declare, "This can be done much better in the following manner."[1] You quickly get tired of people like that.

Jesus isn't out to force all of life to his whim. We recognize people who do such things as having what's called an authoritarian personality. Such people must control everything in the world around them because within them they are so insecure. That's not Jesus. Jesus concentrates here upon the reasons people do religious things.

At the beginning of the last century the American financier J.P. Morgan said, "There are two reasons why a person does anything. There's a good reason, and there's the real reason."[2] Jesus knows the human heart. He knows our real reasons, so he states, "Where your treasure is, there your heart will be also" (v. 21). He puts his finger on what J.P. Morgan noticed and what the poet T.S. Eliot indicts as, "the greatest treason," which is "to do the right thing for the wrong reason."[3]

Jesus isn't attempting to frighten us into an emotional jumble, constantly worried about our every motive. He's not trying to do what happened when a fellow on the ground watched a tightrope walker practice. He looked up, "How do you do that?" The tightrope walker looked down, "I practice a lot and I've got this pole." "Yes, I see that," he said. "But how do you really, really do that?" The tightrope walker put one hand on his chin said, "Well…." and fell off.

Jesus knows our hearts, thus he knows we'll never perfectly understand the Christian faith or have perfect motives. He doesn't want to unhinge us like that unfortunate tightrope walker or like those sad Christians who every minute take their spiritual temperature to see how they're doing with God. Jesus isn't binding us, but freeing us; and, above all it's important to know why Jesus does so.

Maybe you remember the musical "The Man of la Mancha"? It's a rewriting of Cervantes' novel *Don Quixote* mixed with a dramatic retelling of Cervantes' life and folded into a musical. Don Quixote was Cervantes' character, written in the seventeenth-century Spain. The novel has Quixote so addled by tales of chivalry that he sets off with his neighbor, Sancho Panza, to bring justice to the world. Most people know about his jousting with the windmill in the novel and today most everyone recognizes the song, "The Impossible Dream" from the musical. There's another song in the musical, almost forgettable unless you've been in the production yourself. It's titled "I Really Like Him," and that's the bulk of its lyrics — a dull, even insipid, song for what appears to be a pedestrian, ordinary reason. People write thousands of love songs. The radio wears us out with them. How many "like" songs have you heard? The sidekick Sancho sings his "like" song about this rather crazy self-proclaimed knight. And as moderate as the song sounds, it explains why Sancho sticks with Quixote and suffers all kind of indignities because of him.

Sancho likes him. Because he does, in the novel Don Quixote and Sancho Panza talk all the time. They might frustrate one another, but they talk mile after mile on their strange quest. When you like someone, you want to be with them and talk with them. Pretty soon you find yourself devoted to one another. A multitude of marriages have come about that way.

Here's the reason that Jesus tells us to drop our religious phoniness: God likes us. Sounds pretty underwhelming; yet, as I've counseled with people, Christians often don't think that God really likes them or wants to be around them. They might assent to some general belief that God loves them. But that doesn't always affect them. How about thinking of Jesus singing this song about you, "I Really Like You." Has somebody said that to you? Maybe it was from the opposite sex, and maybe you were younger. What would happen if Jesus just showed up with you now — say in worship, in prayer, or even a dream or vision — and spoke your name and added, "I really like *you*."

When you really like someone, you spend your time, energy, and emotion with them. If I really like my wife, I tell her. I don't stand in the grocery store parking lot announcing it to every customer.

If we aim our religious actions merely to be seen by others, Jesus says we've been paid in full. We submit our religious bill to those around us, and they pay us with their admiration. God isn't included in the transaction. Jesus refers to this as where our treasure is. Where we turn our entire attention, that's where our heart will be also. Jesus invites us to live with God through all things and to trust that God likes us. Then we'll want to talk with God about all things.

When we look at our lives from this perspective, we figure out why Jesus uses such strong speech here in the Sermon on the Mount. If Jesus seems tough on us, insisting upon our having the right reasons, it's because so much is at stake: our genuine relationship with God.

Another variation on Cervantes' character of Don Quixote is a book by Graham Greene titled *Monsignor Quixote*, set in Spain just before the death of the dictator Franco, which was 1975. It ends after a journey around Spain with a modern day "descendant," he says, of Don Quixote and his friend, whom he calls "Sancho." Monsignor Quixote, a Roman Catholic priest, normally a mild and kindly man, is infuriated to realize that in a religious procession the honor of carrying a statue of the Virgin Mary, with money from the faithful pinned to it, goes to those who paid the most. The highest bidder gets the prime spot of carrying in the front. The monsignor tries to stop the procession and begins to rip the money from the statue. This should remind us of Jesus' flipping over tables of moneychangers in the temple. Our devotion to God alone is that important. As Monsignor Quixote protests, he's hit in the head. Soon his friend Sancho drives him away from the church while the Civil Guard shoots at his car. Monsignor Quixote dies the next day.

I cite this fictional attempt to portray Quixote because the author, Graham Greene was a devout Roman Catholic. He attempted in modern garb to demonstrate how important it is for Christians to respond to God as we would to anyone else who is devoted to us.

When Jesus was alive he summoned people to believe as he did that God likes us, wants to share our lives, and is devoted to us. It's hard for humans to believe that. It helps us to see evidence in this world that God values us so highly.

Rick Hoyt was born with cerebral palsy, having no control over his arms, legs, or tongue, but his family included him in every activity. He learned to operate a computer by head movements in order to communicate. He was able to graduate from high school and in 1993 from college. While in school he heard an announcement for a benefit run. A cross country athlete had become a paraplegic in an accident. Rick communicated with his father that he would like to participate. His father Dick pushed him in a two wheel running chair.

When they returned home, Rick was connected to his head switch to type on the computer. He told his dad that the joy he had in those five kilometers gave him the feeling that he wasn't handicapped.

His dad began getting into shape to push him in races and learned to swim so they could participate in Ironman races: Dick swimming and towing Rick on a raft behind him, then Dick bicycling with Rick connected to Dick's special bike, then Dick running, pushing Rick in a running chair. As of August 31, 2008, they had completed 229 Triathlons, 66 Marathons, and hundreds of shorter races. Their best time in a triathlon Ironman competition was thirteen and a half hours. You might be interested to know that the father, Dick, is 68 years old.[4]

Sometimes we need a startling demonstration to see how much someone likes us, which we now have with Jesus' death and resurrection. In Jesus God has been on a quest to find us and free us to respond wholeheartedly. God has found us in the handicap of our sin and loved us, or "liked" us if that makes more sense to you. Maybe the message of Jesus' death for us seems a little crazy or weak as the apostle Paul said. Or maybe it's the impossible dream come true that finally focuses all our devotion to God.

Communion

The only good reason to come to communion is also the only good reason that we pray: God wants us to. However, no matter your motivation, God loves you and invites you to this table. Come now and allow Christ's grace not only to purify your motives but also to strengthen you to live his kind of life. Amen.

---

1. Jeremy Bernstein, "The Merely Very Good," in Cynthia Ozick, ed., *The Best American Essays 1998* (Boston: Houghton Mifflin, 1998), p. 40.
2. Jean Strouse, "The Real Reasons," in William Zinsser, ed. *Extraordinary Lives: The Art and Craft of American Biography* (New York: American Heritage, 1986), p. 163.

3. T.S. Eliot, *The Complete Poems and Plays* (New York: Harcourt, Brace and Company, 1934), p. 196.
4. www.teamhoyt.com.

Jesus Tempted in Us

It's good to be here with you. Ten days ago my wife and I were visiting our daughter and son-in-law in central Mexico. In Mexico City they took us to the National Palace in which hangs a painting of Miguel Hidalgo y Costilla. I'm intrigued by this painting. Hidalgo was leader in the Mexican war for independence from Spain; but, by the time people wanted a portrait of him, he was dead. Half a century later Joaquin Ramirez painted a picture of him but used his own brother's face.

The face of one's brother as the leader for independence is a good way to consider Jesus. Jesus has the face of our true brother (or "sister" if you want to think of him that way — that wouldn't bother Jesus). Not that Jesus is "just like one of us." That's not how it works. Our Christian faith has a long history of making Jesus into the person we are, just like us — Democrat if we're Democrats, Republican if we're Republicans, capitalist if we're capitalists, communist if we're communists. That's not the way Jesus has our true brother's face. We can try herding Jesus into the small corral of our little ideas; yet Jesus keeps showing up, instead, as our true brother, trying to free us to live for God. Jesus isn't always what we expect or what we want, but Jesus our true brother brings God to us and us to God. We see in this morning's text how Jesus is our true brother when he's tempted.

We usually think of temptations as Satan trying to get us to do what's wrong. I always remember the pastor and his wife in the 1930s. They lived on almost nothing. One day the pastor comes home and here's his wife in this gorgeous dress. "Where'd you get that dress?"

"Bought it today," she says sheepishly.

"How much did it cost?"

"Ten dollars."

"Ten dollars!" the pastor smacks his head with his hand. "We don't have that kind of money."

The wife looks down and says quietly, "I know, but the devil made me to do it."

"When that happens," the pastor shouts, "you're supposed to say, 'Get behind me, Satan.' "

"I did," she says. "And he said, 'Looks good from back here too.' "

That's not quite the same as Jesus' temptations. The devil isn't struggling every time to get Jesus to do what's completely wrong so much as to do some things for the wrong reason. It's a struggle! The word "temptation" in the New Testament also means a trial or a struggle. Matthew chapter 4 records a lot of spiritual struggle going on in this deserted spot of Palestine. Because Jesus is our brother, he's out in the wilderness struggling against Satan on our behalf. Jesus didn't just die for us. He was born for us, was baptized for us, and was tempted for us. Jesus is the person who lived for God and others. He's doing this for us.

These stories of Jesus' struggle with Satan aren't recorded so we'll admire Jesus, but so Jesus' Spirit may become active in our lives now and so the pattern of Jesus' life becomes the pattern in ours. "Because he himself was tested by what he suffered," the book of Hebrews says, "he is able to help those who are being tested" (Hebrews 2:18). Because the risen Jesus lives in us, every temptation we endure is a temptation of Jesus in us. Jesus' defeating the devil early in his public ministry becomes a present reality when scripture is read and preached, when we listen to his Spirit in our heart, and also when we listen to the testimony of Christian history.

Consider some Christians who've been tempted with Jesus. Jesus' first struggle was to meet his immediate needs instead of trusting God: "You hungry?" Satan said. "Just turn these stones into bread." Albert Schweitzer earned doctorates in theology, philosophy, and music. He was renowned in each discipline. He was on the road to further achievement and greater acclaim. But he read the gospels about our true brother Jesus. He returned to college for six years to become a medical doctor. Then Doctor, Doctor, Doctor, Doctor Schweitzer went to the unhealthiest climate in the world to care for the neediest of the earth's people.

Friends thought he was crazy. The established church wouldn't honor his ministry because of his unorthodox views. But the Paris Mission Society ceded a site for his hospital on the Ogowe[1] River in what was French Equatorial Africa (now Gabon). There in the African jungle he worked out his belief in "the reverence for life." He built, equipped, and maintained the hospital with royalties from his books and proceeds of organ recitals and lectures on visits to Europe. His life commitment was to sacrifice his own needs, even his higher needs for art, by obeying Jesus Christ. Albert Schweitzer received the Nobel Prize for Peace in 1952, which he used to build a leprosarium.

Our Lord Jesus helped him to live not for his own needs but to live for God alone and learn reverence for life beyond himself. In Albert Schweitzer Jesus conquered Satan's first temptation again.

Jesus' second temptation was to perform a spectacular miracle to save himself and to tempt God to come to his beck and call. "Come on, Jesus, leap off this pinnacle. God'll catch you and you'll amaze the crowds." Jesus was challenged to tell God exactly what to do, and if God didn't come through, obviously God wasn't very powerful. Dietrich Bonhoeffer was born in Germany 31 years after Schweitzer. He decided early in life to be a theologian, and so he did, although he was by his own description overly critical, self-righteous, and unloving.

The rise of the Nazis matured him as a Christian. He saw clearly from the beginning that Nazism (any "-ism," "Americanism" included) is an idol. The day after Hitler finally stole what the German electorate would not give him, Bonhoeffer's sermon on the radio was cut off. He fled to the United States for a year, studying at Union Theological Seminary in New York. But he was compelled to return to Germany to oppose Hitler's attempt to rule even the church.

In 1933, again to escape the Nazis, Bonhoeffer went to London to minister to a German congregation. But once more he returned to Germany to help in the struggle against Hitler. He ran an illegal seminary for two years before it was closed by the Gestapo, and again he fled to the United States. But his conscience forced him to return to Germany to continue struggling for the faith of his countrymen. He weaseled his way into German counterintelligence. With a number of his family he joined the plot to assassinate Hitler. For two years he worked for the allies as a double agent until the bomb to kill Hitler didn't, and the list of conspirators was discovered. Bonhoeffer spent two years in Gestapo interrogation camps.

In the prison years Bonhoeffer finally accepted that he'd never be freed. No miracle would come. He, his brother, brother-in-law, and uncle were all executed. Bonhoeffer was hanged April 9, 1945, a few days before the allies liberated his prison camp. But in prison he was a free child of God, just as free as he was three times to go back to his own people to struggle against idolatry, free to be chaplain to his fellow prisoners and to the soldiers who guarded him, free to learn patience and compassion and the depths of God's mercy for all — with or without a miraculous delivery, and free finally to walk to the hangman's rope trusting Jesus Christ.

Jesus was tempted to ask God for a flashy miracle. For Dietrich Bonhoeffer no miracle came, but Jesus again conquered the devil's second temptation.

Jesus' third temptation was to clutch at political power and to use Satan's means to God's ends. Power always tempts us to use it for less than divine goals, which means worshiping Satan instead of God. Dag Hammarskjold was born in Sweden a year earlier than Bonhoeffer. For the last eight and a half years of his life he was Secretary General of the United Nations.

Hammarskjold was raised in a Lutheran home but lost his childhood faith at the university. He studied law and economics and became a civil servant. He never married and lived with his parents as often as he could until he was forty. He wasn't a gregarious man but an extremely hard worker. He was lonely and felt alienated from God, from himself, and from others. He began reading Albert Schweitzer's *The Quest of the Historical Jesus* and meditating upon the gospels.

He had an experience that prepared him for the task soon to be his. He described it: "I don't know Who — or What — put the question, I don't know when it was put. I don't even remember answering. But at some moment I did answer YES to Someone — or Something — and from that hour I was certain that existence is meaningful and that, therefore, my life, in self-surrender, had a goal."[2] So, on New Year's Day 1953, he wrote: "For all that has been — Thanks! For all that shall be — Yes!"[3]

None of this was public. Hammarskjold seldom spoke of the quiet, inward revolution. But no one saw Jesus in the wilderness being tempted by Satan; all they saw was a man who came away to serve God and love others no matter what.

Dag Hammarskjold died in a plane crash September 17, 1961, in Africa, while trying to negotiate peace in the

Belgian Congo. After his death beside his bed a journal was found that recorded his deepest thoughts for 36 years. It revealed to the world the struggle to come to mature faith, and it showed the burden upon one who has power to be concerned for others instead of for oneself.

He was posthumously awarded the Nobel Prize for Peace and his diary was printed with the title: *Markings.* He died carrying in his pocket a copy of Thomas á Kempis' ancient book, *The Imitation of Christ,* and as a bookmark, a postcard on which was typed his oath of office as Secretary General of the United Nations. He set out not to dominate the world but to serve it. In him our Lord Jesus Christ was beating Satan for the third time.

Three examples of Jesus still being tested in Christians — and my students call these three examples "old white men." But Jesus is present within all who trust him, no matter if we are white as a sheet, brown as our son-in-law, or purple with pink stripes. Jesus our brother summons us into God's life and service no matter the continent we live upon or the private basketful of prejudices we use to judge the rest of humanity.

We are always tempted to use Jesus, make him into anything we want in order to justify our self-concern. So, notice this about Jesus: Before he went to the wilderness he knew the scriptures. Jesus knew what God was like. We need to know the scriptures to see what Jesus is like, spend time with him so we can differentiate his leading from the deceitful voice of evil. Our first task as Christians is to ponder Jesus so that he begins to turn us into his image instead of each of us trying to convert him into a little clone of me.

I think of Jesus' presence working itself into our lives when I remember all the jade we saw in Mexico's National Museum of Anthropology. We inspected gorgeous jade pieces. Because jade is so valuable, people over the centuries have sought to become experts in identifying the best pieces.

The story is passed on about a man determined to learn to select jade. He found the greatest expert in the land and told him he wanted to learn to evaluate jade. The expert agreed, said it would take six days a week work for six months and they settled on the price.

First day the student comes to the expert's precious gems warehouse and the expert puts him in a room alone, sets him in a chair at a table, and plops down a piece of jade in front of him. He says, "This is a good piece." Nothing else all day. Next day the expert comes in and sets down another jade and says, "This is a poor piece." Nothing changes for six months, only the expert every morning putting a chunk of jade on the table and proclaiming it good or poor.

After six months the student files a civil suit, brings his teacher to court, and explains to the judge that his teacher hasn't taught him to select jade. The teacher is then led into court. He's carrying a piece of jade. As the teacher walks to the witness stand, he steps over to the student and puts a piece of jade in the student's hand.

The student stands up in a rage. "Your honor," he says, "right here in front of you is all the evidence you need. See. This man I hired to be my teacher did that every day, brought a piece and put it in my hand, and as you can see, this is a very poor piece."

Spend time with Jesus. Let him consciously and unconsciously sink into your life. He's a great deal like you, but he wants you to be more like him. Get to know him by meditating upon the gospels. Watch what he does. Listen to what he says. He's living again within Christians, we who are ordinary or those who are extraordinary. Schweitzer, Bonhoeffer, Hammarskjold, you: God still overcomes temptations for those who open themselves to the living Jesus within us. If you are in Jesus, Jesus is your true brother, struggling again to free you to live as he did — for God and others.

Communion

Our Lord Jesus invites you to this table to share his life and strength. Here he makes us strong to live for him and wise to flee temptation. Amen.

_____

1. Also spelled: Ogooue.
2. Dag Hammarskjold, Markings (New York: Knopf, 1964), p. 205.
3. Hammarskjold, p. 89.

Lent 2
John 3:1-17

Nicodemus: A Young Old Man

Sermon Note: This story sermon is best read with a "special" voice reserved for the scripture included in the story. Read the scripture with a lower and slower voice so that the congregation realizes that all the rest is the story is "commentary" on the scripture.

When the last farmer from the most distant field arrived home to his family and the temple police were tromping their patrols around Jerusalem's walls and the remaining member of the Sanhedrin set aside the last legal brief and blew out the seven candles at the entrance of the Sanhedrin's chambers, Nicodemus left his quarters. He looked quickly left, then right, and walked out into the night. The first blast of wind hit him around a corner like icicles flying sideways. He jerked his cloak tight.

To anyone passing, this old man, robed with dignity, could be a physician out tending the ill or a scribe returning from a late session of teaching a convert's family. The night can disguise identity and motive. It can even obscure a man's hesitant gait.

Nicodemus was one of 6,000 Pharisees, the separated ones, the religious elite. He was one of seventy who constituted the Sanhedrin that, with the consent of the Romans, shared in the rule of their country. He was a renowned teacher, deferred to for decisions requiring extra wisdom or breadth of experience, and he was master of a great fortune; yet, he walked the street, covering his face in his robe, which served for more than merely struggling against the cold.

He knew where Jesus was staying. As he neared Jesus' house, his chest seemed like a cave full of crazed bats. What's so disturbing about this young man? Is it because, unlike the scribes, Jesus doesn't lay down his main proposition, as a general sends his infantry into the field, and then Jesus doesn't surround that proposition with quotes from the esteemed rabbis, as a general rings his troops with wings of cavalry?

Two men approached at a distance. Nicodemus dashed into an alley and walked faster. The wind curled under his cloak and he clung more tightly. Is it because of Jesus' freedom with the law, challenging all, yet not like one of those men-haters who claim a prophetic calling in order to shout cruel things to others? Or is it his eyes — looking at evil and making it wither, looking at obedience and inspiring greater devotion? Or is it the eyes of those Jesus cured, eyes that moments before revealed long vacant halls of rejection and suffering, now lit like two lamps burning in the holy temple?

Such thoughts kept Nicodemus awake and tossing every night for a week. He heard the young rabbi teach and saw him heal people. And old Nicodemus had ducked behind a pillar when the Galilean chased money-changers from the temple, splattering their bowls of coins and sending merchants scampering down the temple steps, chasing their animals.

There Jesus stood when they'd all escaped ahead of him, outlined like a statue, square at the temple's southern entrance, in his hand the whip of cords dangling limp to the floor. What gave him such authority? Why did even the temple police withdraw as a pack of wolves that discovered its quarry stronger than expected?

Now there was a Pharisee named Nicodemus, a leader of the Jews. He came to Jesus by night (v. 1). Nicodemus, shaking off the last shiver of reluctance, rapped at the door. The soft steps inside became louder, and the one who'd chased people from the temple now filled this doorway. But his eyes that before had invited strangers seemed merciful still and Nicodemus stepped out of the dark.

Seated comfortably in the house, the Galilean builder waited, his silence being an unspoken question to the white-haired man whose breathing from the long walk was returning to normal. *"Rabbi,"* he said to Jesus, *"we know that you are a teacher who has come from God; for no one can do these signs that you do apart from the presence of God"* (v. 2). Nicodemus started the safe way — with God. Make a statement about theology and if Jesus can enlighten you, then it's almost worth coming; but, if he can't detect the deeper intent, the question behind the statement, the fear behind the face, then depart quickly to arrive home before the wind blows more bitterly. If Jesus can't sense the searing heart problem, Nicodemus will dismiss his suspicions about the man's powers. He'll return, almost relieved, to his sad, old world, yielding to his original faith as threadbare as it is, assuming that faith can't do much more for anyone.

Jesus answered him, "Very truly, I tell you, no one can see the kingdom of God without being born from above" (v. 5). If Nicodemus was confused in coming, if his perception of Galilee's prophet was like a balance teetering between fascination and doubt, now his balance didn't seem able to weigh anything of what Jesus said. The first piece on his mind's chessboard was taken by the young man as easily as Nicodemus had swept a real chessboard when he taught his son the game. Nicodemus was now in *this* game to the end.

Nicodemus said to him, "How can anyone be born after having grown old? Can one enter a second time into the mother's womb and be born?" (v. 4). Nicodemus was old, not just physically old, he'd grown spiritually old. He didn't catch Jesus' play on the word that meant both "from above" and "again." With the continued Roman occupation, his hope for a free Israel had waned. Serving on the Sanhedrin and hearing endless disputes over possessions and power, he lost his broad love for people. As his fortune grew, his compassion for the unfortunate died. Then Tamar died. Married since she was fifteen and he was seventeen, he always said, "We grew up together." Now, the wife of his youth, the mother of his children, lay in the family tomb ready for Nicodemus a year after her death to gather her bones into a stone box.

Everything seemed old within him — tired, used up. The joints of his very spirit complained in pain. Yet he responded to Jesus. Something burned dimly within him. Something puffed upon that ember of faith inside him and maybe a flame would yet leap up.

Whatever stirred was akin to his feelings a year and a half ago when John the Baptist moved among the people as a fox through the chickens, chasing everyone off their religious nests, challenging even the best people to humility and repentance. But Herod Antipas had been out to get John and Nicodemus knew he would.

Jesus answered, "Very truly, I tell you, no one can enter the kingdom of God without being born of water and Spirit. What is born of the flesh is flesh, and what is born of the Spirit is spirit. Do not be astonished that I said to you, 'You must be born from above'" (vv. 5-6). Jesus paused. Such a direct and uncompromising challenge hit Nicodemus like a rock from a catapult. If forced to say so, he'd admit that his faith was crippled, his hope blunted, his love as empty as a pond in a drought. His spirit was numb, his mind paralyzed, and now this young Nazarene simply reached into Nicodemus's life. More than merely pointing to the aching spot, Jesus laid his hand exactly on the raw and bleeding slice of Nicodemus's soul and made it burn all the more.

A gust of wind rattled the door and Jesus continued, *"The wind blows where it chooses, and you hear the sound of it, but you do not know where it comes from or where it goes. So it is with everyone who is born of the Spirit"* (v. 9).

Nicodemus's mind sifted through fragments of thoughts and feelings. *I know something's dead that should come to life within me, but how? How could God breathe into my life? The roads to the past are closed as surely as the gate to Eden's garden. What wind from God can blow me toward joy again, toward hope and love again?*

Nicodemus sighed. Jesus had confirmed that Nicodemus was a half-stamped coin, a piece of pottery poorly thrown. But how in God's world could this ever change? All humanity experienced birth and growth, aging and death. Sometimes pestilence, famine, or war cut life off prematurely as a knife slicing short the burning rope of time. But, never had it been reversed. Fine to talk about God's Spirit, but God's Spirit had never — until then anyway — never turned a tottering, white-haired man to a lithe, black-haired youth. No elderly, shriveled muscles had learned again to play follow-the-leader or hide-and-seek, to leap ditches, to jump from walls, or to annoy merchants by playing tag all morning through the marketplace.

Nicodemus said to him, "How can these things be?" Jesus answered him, "Are you a teacher of Israel, and yet you do not understand these things?" (vv. 9-10). Nicodemus half-closed his eyes. How could he start over, he who studied the scriptures until his eyes ached? Had he missed something important, the center of Israel's law, the middle of God's revelation to the Hebrews?

Jesus talked on, but Nicodemus caught only a few words. In his memory he was unrolling the scroll of the law as a merchant unrolled his rug every morning under his awning. He had placed these texts in his heart years before. With the other students he'd gratefully leaned over the holy scrolls. Now, from the scriptures what is foremost? What is primary in them? What is central that all the rest lead to, as spokes to a hub?

God's dealings with Israel passed before him: God's loving offers, Israel's mistakes, God's gracious corrections, Israel's new attempts at obedience that led to other failures. And what of the law *he* practiced? Was the Pharisees' minute and careful observing of the law God's goal for everyone? Was his life's commitment truly on the trail to God's kingdom, or was his whole life traveling into a box canyon?

Then he caught Jesus' phrase, *"For God so loved the world that he gave his only Son, so that everyone who believes in him may not perish but may have eternal life"* (John 3:16). Nicodemus was check-mated in three moves. He sat like a cobra at the end of a charmer's pipe. Nicodemus who everyone else considered the capable, the strong, the successful — *this* Nicodemus had lost, and how wonderful the defeat was. He felt the gentle miracle enfold him as the strong mystery of Jesus' authority overwhelmed him. Of course he couldn't force his ideas to fit with Jesus' teaching. Jesus wasn't going to change and his message wouldn't change. Nicodemus sat knee to knee with God's supreme gift. In a long line of gifts to a stumbling world that didn't deserve them, now God fulfilled all promises in this son.

Nicodemus was slow to walk, slow to change, but he left Jesus' house that night feeling almost as young as he was speechless — as one feels who escapes alive from Herod's throne room. He'd met a greatness that was disorienting and uncompromising — not uncompromising in anger but in the certainty of God's love.

With his frail, decrepit hope and tattered, routine faith he left Jesus and walked into the night, but not as he came. The night didn't seem as dark. He didn't even think about anyone's seeing him leave Jesus' house. Dusk had hushed the land long before, but Nicodemus's mind swirled with thoughts not about the sundown but of a new dawn.

He'd accept the birth from above. But he needed time, as a prince needs time to assess the damage a storm has caused a province. He'd be awake all night again, not sorting through his doubts, or reliving the lonely agony of Tamar's death, but sifting through the evening's conversation, trying to understand better what happened in talking with Jesus.

Ahead in the dim light of a moon no longer obscured, a gust of wind gathered a wave of dust. It set him back a step as it swept down the street. Jesus' words returned, *"The wind blows where it chooses, and you hear the sound of it, but you do not know where it comes from or where it goes. So it is with everyone who is born of the Spirit"* (v. 8). The Spirit held much in store for young-old Nicodemus. He'd find changes to make in every direction he turned. Later he defended Jesus before the Sanhedrin, not well, but he made his start. Finally, he helped Joseph of Arimathea bury Jesus.

No one knows what he thought when Jesus died or if he buried Jesus with or without hope. But perhaps as he placed Jesus in the tomb he prayed that the mighty Spirit that changed an aged, tired, grieving heart to begin to love and hope would again do something wonderful, even with the death of God's only Son.

Communion

Our Lord Jesus invites everyone to his table, the doubting and the confident, the grieving and the joyful, and the young and the old. Jesus even invites the old young and the young old. Here, while sharing Jesus' meal, the wind of God's Spirit blows into our lives. Who knows where it came from? In the short run, who knows where it will take us? In the long run we trust that it will lead us all the way to God. Amen.

The Bridge at Sychar

A great deal of the Bible is quite understandable by itself. To grasp much of the Bible we don't need tons of background, familiarity with ancient languages, or an advanced degree in archaeology. Then we approach other passages where we need the collective wisdom from the church's scholars to open up the fuller meaning.

We're at such a place today. John chapter 4 speaks much louder of God's grace when we review some background information. First, the history between the Jews and Samaritans was vicious, with grievous wrongs having been committed by both groups. Second, this text is full of puns that aren't obvious in an English translation. Consequently, reading English we don't understand why the woman doesn't immediately catch the drift of Jesus' words. Third, we need to know — without too many gory details — that nearly everyone at Jesus' time could offer half a dozen reasons why he shouldn't be talking to this woman.

When we delve into the customs of the day, we find that her coming to draw water at noon is a giveaway that she's a social outcast. Women drew the water but certainly not at noon in the heat of the day. She's a Samaritan woman who's an outcast of the Samaritan village, yet the Samaritans as a whole are outcasts from the Jews. So, we've got one ethnic community (the Jews) that throws out what it considers its human garbage (the Samaritans) and that community then points to one of the lowest people on their social register: this woman.

Jesus' conversation with the woman is scandalous. We catch a glimpse of this opinion when Jesus' students return and the scripture says, "They were astonished that he was speaking with a woman" (v. 27).

Jesus reaches out to a person who's least valued in her community. A friend of mine used to say that if Jesus came to our town today, he'd be driving a beat-up, old pick-up truck and the first place he'd go is the tavern. It's Jesus' style as we read the gospels. You'd certainly never guess that by looking at what's become of his church. Don't we all look nice and proper? Jesus, however, reaches out to everyone, not just by what he says, but literally by what he does.

This isn't just Jesus' style. It's also the main theme of the Bible. We don't work our way to God by being good, studying religion, or even seeking God. No matter how we view it from our perspective, the Bible tells the true story: God searches for us. In the Bible God always reaches out to us first. God takes the initiative. So, here at a well in Samaria Jesus isn't just crossing ethnic, religious, moral, or even sexual boundaries. Through Jesus God is reaching out across all eternity.

The city of Istanbul, Turkey, sits on two continents: Asia and Europe. In 1973, the first Bosphorus Bridge linked the two halves of the city, connecting the two continents permanently for the first time in history. Think of Jesus as that kind of bridge, spanning from eternity to time, from heaven to earth, from God to us. Through Jesus God is reaching out to humanity, bridging the gap between us. Jesus sits down outside the ancient village of Sychar, but where he meets the woman isn't just a well. It's a bridge.

The woman doesn't understand what's going on until later. Jesus' students also don't catch the meaning of the encounter. We, however, have the entire gospel of John and the rest of the New Testament to help evaluate the significance of Jesus' meeting with a Samaritan. God's offer to humanity is wrapped up in Jesus' conversation with this woman on heaven's bridge.

Notice how Jesus links us to God. Jesus focuses only upon the person he talks with. Even in a crowd Jesus can aim his attention to one person at a time. He's never just doing something in general or for symbolic effect. He's genuinely and specifically relating to this one woman whom others, even of her own outcast ethnic group, don't respect.

In this case, Jesus makes contact with a request, "Give me a drink" (v. 7). Then they chat about water, wells, springs, and worship, which was pretty natural stuff at the time. The more arid the region the more important water is. Plus, as stilted or artificial as the discussion about water seems, we know from the Dead Sea Scrolls that other people at the time spoke in such symbols about worship and God.

Jesus asks for a drink. He's not afraid of her or her sin. She's important enough to give him a drink and to engage in a conversation about life's ultimate concerns. We can put ourselves in her place and realize that on the receiving end of a conversation with Jesus, yes, we recognize our sinfulness, as does Peter when Jesus in the boat with him tells him to let down his nets for a catch. A whole night already fishing and they've caught nothing, but obeying Jesus, they catch so much the boat starts to sink. When Peter figures out what's going on he falls on his knees and says, "Go away from me, Lord, for I am a sinful man!" (Luke 5:8).

An uncomfortable awareness of our sin is one response to meeting Jesus. Yet, that's never the last thing we realize. Jesus, as with Peter and here with the woman, goes beyond our sinfulness to our essential value with God. Jesus wouldn't be here if God didn't love us. That is what's most important to understand because when it finally sinks into us that God loves us, we not only change our minds about God but about ourselves.

John Calvin was a forebear of our Presbyterian approach to the Bible and the Christian faith. Basically he said in his gigantic *Institutes of the Christian Religion* that of all there is to know about life, the most important are 1) to know about God and 2) to know about ourselves. Learning that God is our creator means that we aren't a speck of dust free floating in a meaningless universe. Learning, as does the Samaritan woman, that Jesus is God's emissary of eternal life restores us to our true place as creatures granted the very image of God upon us.

A few people think too much of themselves, and they're certainly irritating to be around. But most of us think too little of ourselves and the rotten things we do to ourselves and others is because we think so poorly of ourselves. Adolph Eichmann was an example in Germany. He lost a job as an oil salesman in the Depression and failed as a vacuum cleaner salesman. Finally he linked up with the German SS and eventually headed the Nazi effort to find and murder Europe's Jews. As a failure he settled for being a servile bureaucrat who, though having nothing personally against Jews, performed a job that diluted his sense of right and wrong and ended in mass executions that slaughtered millions.

It's when we feel like horrible losers that we act like horrible losers. Christians don't have to become like the ultra secularists who worship self-esteem. Yet, we must realize that humans need a sense of dignity. We're created with it, and without it we feel, if not act, like we and others are without value.

Pulitzer Prize winning author Alice Walker tells that, when she was eight, she was shot in the eye with a BB gun and that eye was blinded. Besides being blind, the injury caused a permanent, messy scar in her eye. She instantly went from being a bright, happy child to a miserable one, taunted by other children and feeling wretched. For the next six years, she says, she didn't look anyone in the eye because she never raised her head. She hated her eye, and when she was alone she ranted at it. She carried this inferior feeling all her life — a damaged eye that sometimes rolled without her control. She regained some of her poise when surgery at fourteen removed most of the eye's ugly scar. But inside she wasn't healed.

When she gave birth to a daughter, she wondered what would happen when the child realized her mother's eye was different. When the child was almost three, she regularly watched the television show "Big Blue Marble," named for what the earth looked like from the moon. One day when putting her daughter to sleep, her daughter focused on her blind eye. Alice Walker wrote that she felt it coming, that someday her child would realize her mother's eye was different and would say something hurtful to her. Instead, her daughter said in amazement, "Mommy, there's a *world* in your eye," and she asked how it got there.[1]

It took someone who loved Alice Walker completely, unconditionally, to see a wonderful world where others saw only injury or disability, someone who accepted her as she was and thought she was beautiful. Not all of Walker's problems were settled there, but a whole bunch were.

Jesus arrives across the bridge from heaven to meet the Samaritan woman at the well. He expresses to her God's unconditional regard, God's ultimate concern for her. Sure, she first feels the sting of her sin, but that passes when Jesus won't give up on her. The woman, as do we all, needs to know about God and about herself. It's as though Jesus says, "You're so important that God sent me to you." Not all of her problems are solved that moment, but a whole bunch are. She heads off to the village to share her imperfect understanding of Jesus, and she's not only on the way to town, she's on the way to recovery as God's beloved creature.

That's what happens when Jesus shows up, meeting us at a well, at work, at a party, or a picnic — even encountering us in worship! Yes, right here and right now Jesus shows up in worship so that our meeting him here is an experience of spirit and truth. Here he totally centers upon us, gives us God's entire attention.

When you talk face-to-face with Jesus, you're in the conversation of a lifetime and beyond. When you talk with Jesus, no one is more important at that moment than you. We don't have to cower because Jesus sees our sins. He's more willing to forgive our sins than we are to confess them. He'll start the conversation with us. He'll even summon us to come to him when we don't quite know what's going on. No matter how tired *he* is, he says, "Come to me, all you that are weary and are carrying heavy burdens, and I will give you rest" (Matthew 11:28).

I like the sign outside the chiropractor's office that says, "Crawl-ins welcome." That's Jesus. He wants us to come to him no matter what we feel like and no matter how we feel about ourselves. He's crossed a great bridge to get to us. Now, no matter what circumstances it takes to get us in a conversation, no matter what others think of us, Jesus sits here looking at us, loving us, and listening to us. He hears our pains and sees our problems, problems maybe we've had since we were eight, or 18, or 28. But he sees beyond them. He gazes into our soul and glimpses this wonderful child God created, able to enjoy the world and love others, and able to contribute to life and spread God's good news. And here's the best: Because Jesus loves us, what he sees in us is what really counts, and what — in his love — we become.

Now we build bridges from Jesus to others. We, like the Samaritan woman, spread the word about Jesus with whatever understanding we have of him. We now gaze into the faces of our families and friends, our neighbors and acquaintances, and see the very image of God waiting for the love of Jesus, awaiting the word about Jesus. That's why Jesus crossed the bridge from heaven to earth: to link us with God, to forgive us, and to love us into the people God created us to be. He's now working through us to restore this big, blue marble of earth to a world of friendship and peace. As we live for Jesus here, we realize that we are taking the first steps with him back across the bridge to heaven.

Communion

It's not just that God reaches out to us first. God reaches out to us always — now through the Holy Spirit. Here at our Lord's table Jesus again reaches to us and hands us God's love in the form of his body broken for us and his blood poured out for us. Those who eat here will never be hungry. Those who drink here will never be thirsty. Amen.

---

1. Alice Walker, "Beauty: When the Other Dancer Is the Self," reprinted in Comley, et al, *Fields of Writing: Readings across the Disciples*, Fourth Edition (New York: St. Martin's Press, 1994), pp. 46-52.

Seeing Jesus

Josiah Harlan was the first American to enter Afghanistan. He did so as a doctor with British Forces. We're not talking about the 1990s, but the 1830s. Harlan was a brilliant, self-absorbed adventurer who'd read a few medical books and passed a cursory exam to be an army surgeon. He later attempted to become an Afghan prince, leading his own army.

No matter his extreme self-importance and self-centeredness, Harlan's abilities as a primitive doctor helped a lot of people. An elderly Afghan woman heard he was a surgeon and approached to ask if he'd operate on her cataracts that had blinded her. He proceeded in the painful surgery and she was instantly able to see. He was about to apply the dressings, but she resisted. She said, "Let me first look upon the face of my deliverer to whom I owe a second creation."[1]

She wanted to *see* the person who'd given her sight. The man born blind in John nine wants to *understand* the person who gave him sight.

Since at the end of John 8 Jesus was near the temple, this whole event with Jesus and the man born blind probably takes place around Jerusalem's temple precincts — about 35 acres that surrounded the actual temple, which itself was a building the size of a gymnasium. The area around the temple was like a small town in that everyone knew everyone else. Today maybe we'd say it had the community of a mall, where most of the regulars can identify the blind beggar. And he, instead of Jesus, becomes the person we hear most about in this incident.

Everyone else recorded here responds to the blind man, starting with Jesus' students. They and the Pharisees accept the popular theology that says that if you're suffering, someone sinned. People around us still mouth such sub-Christian idiocy. A tornado levels a town and the TV crew interviews a devout survivor who asserts for all the world to hear, "God must have a reason." As though God kills people... or causes them to be born blind. People who say such things are basically doing what the Pharisees thought they were doing. They're trying to save God's reputation. Their solution for why people suffer is because they've sinned. Nice and neat and no problem for them about innocent suffering. With that kind of calculation there's no such thing as innocent suffering.

The rest of us are a little more squeamish when blaming God for suffering, but we certainly wonder about it. Why *do* the innocent suffer? Tiny children, babes who've never even had a conscious thought (good or bad), are swept away in a tsunami, blasted by a hurricane, smashed in an earthquake, or slowly starved in a famine — they sinned?

We'd be less than human if we didn't ask why such suffering. But look at what Jesus does while his pious students are inquiring about who sinned to produce this suffering. Jesus, instead, acts. This is a real person who's suffering for crying out loud, and Jesus isn't going to lounge around, chewing over theories, or spouting explanations for suffering. Basically Jesus says, "God's going to work even here." Then he heals the man's eyes in a way the man can understand — spittle was believed to be medicinal. Others mill around chatting about the cause of misery, and Jesus cures it.

We can imagine what the experience was like for this man — a dark world all his life — suddenly coming to light. Voices he'd always heard he can now attach to faces. Maybe he'd even heard what others speculated about the cause of his blindness, heard Jesus' words and then saw, first thing, Jesus' face.

That's where he starts to learn about Jesus. And his learning grows. The man often speaks of not knowing enough about Jesus. He says he doesn't know where Jesus is. He doesn't know if Jesus is a sinner. He doesn't know who the Son of Man is. But throughout he's understanding more about Jesus.

He didn't go looking for healing. Jesus simply seeks him out and heals him. Later Jesus comes looking for him again. So, it didn't start with the blind man's initiative. He was asking for coins, not miracles; but, he's now got something to say about what happened to him and his strained and changing thoughts about Jesus are enough.

A horrible lot of Christians think that in order to share their faith, they need a master's degree in theology or something. Seldom is that necessary. I could almost say (not quite, but almost) that when it comes to sharing your faith, seldom is a master's degree in theology helpful. People who don't know a lot of details about the Christian faith can share what they do know, and like this man, they can share what they've experienced.

Think of musicians. Many musicians, while taking music lessons themselves, also give lessons. You can teach what you know, and you don't have to know a lot more than the person you teach. When it comes to faith, if you have a relationship with God and another person doesn't, you have something to share. When he's interrogated by the religious authorities, the ex-blind man is unsure of himself but states what he knows. Finally they sputter back at him, "Are you trying to teach us?" Well, yes, and so can we with what little or much that we know and experience of Jesus.

Now, first of all we need, as does this man, to be as smart as possible in talking about Jesus. For the sake of our Lord we must think carefully about what we say for him. Often popular religion simply equates feelings with faith. That can be a real problem. If faith can be reduced just to feelings, then the question isn't "Is Jesus the clearest revelation of God in all creation?" but "How do you feel today?"

Our feelings, as a church educator used to say, are friendly. They're part of how God created us. They're just not enough, consistently, to base faith upon. I can feel rotten, sometimes even when I'm serving God in an important way (like informing parents that their child was killed in a car accident), but that doesn't mean God's not with me and helping me do what's difficult.

That said there's a great deal we *can* say about our knowledge and experience of God. As tragically silly as some Christians are, defining the God of the universe by the momentary state of their digestion, more Christians nowadays seem tongue-tied to offer any word on God's behalf, as though they have nothing to utter that could help others to faith. We, like the man born blind, can offer the assessment of what God has been doing in our lives. There's more to say about God than that but at least the man born blind is the expert on his life. We're the experts on our life. We have something to say. An old gospel song summarizes today's Bible text and what we can express in our own words about Jesus, "Once I was blind, but now I can see: The Light of the world is Jesus!"

For every person who pooh-poohs faith and says, "Oh, it's all psychological," there's another person waiting to hear an honest appraisal of how God through all our ups and downs has affected our lives. For every person who says that believers merely look at the sky and wish there was a God, another person needs to hear us say that such reasoning can turn the other direction. Maybe, instead, non-believers look at the sky and wish there wasn't a God!

We each have something we can say — as fragmented as it might be — to help others grow in faith. We get to see the ex-blind man grow in faith and understanding until finally he realizes that Jesus is God's ultimate representative, the Son of Man, and he worships Jesus.

That's the big shift in the story. It's from the man's eyesight to his insight. The whole event is about "seeing" Jesus in two different ways: simple, physical sight and then being able to see what Jesus means.

With the woman Josiah Harlan performed cataract surgery on: She wanted to see the face of the one who cured her. With Jesus we need to discover who he really is. He's not a scoundrel like Harlan who wants to establish his own little kingdom. Jesus expends all his love and energy for God and others and, in John 8, especially for the blind man.

The blind man in his helplessness and confusion is found by Jesus and thus his former suffering puts him a step ahead in understanding Jesus. His suffering wasn't good, but in the end God could use even that for the faith of others. He begins to figure out that Jesus is more than he first appears. He starts to see who Jesus really is.

Jesus grants us the ability to see that life is about living with God for the sake of others. When we look at what Jesus does and listen to what he says, we see God's intention for the world. Consequently, our painful questions about suffering find some relief when Jesus comes on the scene. We know that, since Jesus is God's perfect expression on earth, God doesn't strike humans with suffering; although, life itself usually makes us pay in this world for our mistakes.

Look at the man born blind. When his suffering meets Jesus' compassion it results in God's glory, which means it boosts God's reputation. Jesus, showing us God, doesn't afflict people with pains to match their sins. He heals people and restores us into a new life with God.

Remember how this story begins. Everyone except Jesus crowds around debating "why" a person's suffering. When you've suffered, maybe others have wondered about your sin.... Maybe you've asked yourself if God has struck you in punishment.... In the midst of our suffering, however, Jesus does something about it — outside of us or inside of us. Jesus does something. His questions aren't about why. He asks "What"? What can I do even with this suffering?

In Jesus we won't see God's path crisscrossing roughshod through human suffering. Instead, in Jesus we gaze upon the clearest view of God's heart ever seen.

We won't understand everything about suffering — our personal suffering or others' suffering. We'll still ask our questions. But we'll trust that Jesus has come right out of nowhere to find us and heal us — maybe our body and soul or maybe just our soul for now.

Then Jesus helps us understand enough about God that we can tell others the precious little we know. For it is precious — whether we share it in small towns, big cities, or a mall. And in every human difficulty we can now look and say, "What can we do about this?" When we do, we're imitating God who looks at Jesus crucified outside of old Jerusalem's walls. I imagine it this way. God sadly ponders Jesus' lifeless body and says, "What can I do even with this?"

Communion

If you trust that even with a blind man in Jerusalem Jesus brought sight, if you believe that God even used the horrible miscarriage of justice of Jesus' death for our benefit, then come to the Lord's table and *see* what God can do with this cup and this bread. Amen.

---

1. Ben Macintyre, *Josiah the Great: The True Story of the Man Who Would Be King* (London: HarperCollins, 2004), pp. 67-68.

Where Is Jesus?

For the last few years our family has visited The Dalles, Oregon, for Memorial Day to be with my wife's relatives and to decorate graves in the cemetery. One thing I notice as we visit that cemetery: When you're in the western, older side of the cemetery, visitors are chattier, even happy, carrying on humorous conversations as they stand next to gravestones of people who died a hundred years ago. But, as you enter the newer portion of the cemetery where people have recently been buried, you feel the emotion around. You see families you don't know, but you can tell: the sighs, the hugs, and the tears.

Bereavement hurts, even in the near vicinity of death. So some people never attend funerals and some never visit in hospitals or nursing homes. No matter how they protest they want to remember the person as he or she was, to some extent it's because we all want to avoid the pain of death.

Another way we avoid death's pain is to create gentle terms for dying and the circumstances of death. Funeral homes have "slumber rooms." Instead of saying, "He died," we say, "passed away." Various groups have their own tender expressions, which aren't always understandable to others. I remember my dad's cousin talking about a recent Danish immigrant to North Dakota nearly a hundred years ago. He came into the mercantile one day, all excited, to announce to the gathered farmers that "So and So," one of the farmers in the county, had "popped the pail." For those younger and the non-North Dakotans, he was trying to reproduce the euphemism: "Kicked the bucket."

Also, when we're near the precincts of death, because we're ill at ease with pain and dying, some people nervously, even compulsively, flock around with comforting advice, whether asked for or not. They say things like, "God called him home," or "He's with God now," or "There must be a reason." We've all heard these, probably said them ourselves. We've grown up with them, and they're sincere attempts to help our friends and relatives in their grief. But, without our thinking about it, some of these statements carry the message that God has killed the person. Yes, God has taken the person home to heaven but only after death has released him.

Paul the apostle came along a few years after Jesus' resurrection and perfectly expressed Jesus' life and mission when he advised Christians they should rejoice with those who rejoice but weep with those who weep. For all that we'd like to help others in grief by saying something profound or comforting, usually people in grief need someone to answer the phone or make phone calls for them, to answer the door and get the mail, and especially to drive them somewhere because they're not safe behind the wheel. In grief we much more need someone with us than someone advising us.

Although it's hard the closer we draw toward death to get our thoughts in a neat row, we need to do so here in worship as we study the scriptures. And the clearest way to think about death is first to attend to what Jesus did and did not teach. For all that Jesus taught God's love and challenge, Jesus never taught his students that God plans the earthquake that flattens children in their school. Although Jesus said that God's love follows us to any extreme and that the consequences of our sins must be dealt with, Jesus didn't say that God directs the hurricane that drowns entire villages, nor does God fan the flames that overtake firefighters. If God does such things, then Jesus, God's Son, was only going around fixing what his heavenly Father broke. In the Bible we hear the apostle Paul write that he's having a hard time choosing between remaining in this life or succumbing to death in order to be with his Lord. We take that as a very pious statement — dying to see the Lord. But it's not a cute quip for Paul. Paul stated clearly that death is an enemy. In fact, it's the last enemy yet to be destroyed.

Samuel Johnson, that always interesting eighteenth-century Englishman, said to his biographer Boswell, "When a man knows he is to be hanged in a fortnight, it concentrates his mind wonderfully." If that doesn't happen exactly, at least death makes us intent; because our thoughts and emotions can become fuzzy in the presence of death. If death doesn't always concentrate our thinking, it certainly concentrates our attention. I've called on families in hospitals attending their dying loved ones. Days or weeks slide by, sirens wail at the Emergency Room, Lent comes and Easter goes, the family is unaware. Their world shrinks around their loved one. And in that tiny, painful space, just as we wonder when we approach the newer graves in the cemetery, they ask out loud or silently: "Where is God in this?" Near the pain and mystery of death we falter. I remember the bumper sticker, "There is no hope. But I might be wrong." In the hospital, often in an emotional jumble, no matter a person's faith, the bumper sticker changes to: "I thought there was hope. But I might be wrong."

Maybe some stern, super-religious person declares you second rate because, when nearing death, your faith flickers with a weaker light. Jesus is more merciful. We see him today arriving in Bethany, just over the Mount of Olives, a couple of miles east of Jerusalem. Jesus' friend Lazarus has died, and we hear that Jesus loves him and his sisters Mary and Martha.

Lazarus has *died*. His sisters Mary and Martha believed there *was* hope. Now they wonder if they were wrong. Four days since Lazarus died and where was Jesus when they sent for him?

49

Mary and Martha greet Jesus with the same words, "Lord, if you had been here, my brother would not have died" (v. 21). Jesus responds to Martha, "I am the resurrection and the life" (v. 25). Jesus means right now, right where he stands with Martha, as a person he is resurrection life. He as a human being is God's very life on earth. So we watch him and see what he does and the first and most obvious is that, although Jesus doesn't show up when and where we think he should, he does come to Mary and Martha, to Lazarus and to us.

The gospel of John is careful to tell us that, when Jesus sees Lazarus' sister crying, "He was greatly disturbed in spirit," meaning in the original New Testament that he has "an intense, strong feeling of concern."[1] Then the gospel records Jesus was "deeply moved." In the original that expresses "an acute emotional distress or turbulence."[2] Finally, if it's not enough that John tells us how Jesus feels, John records that shortest verse of the Bible as the New Revised Standard Version translates it, "Jesus began to weep" (v. 35). Old English translations rendered this, "Jesus wept." But that's overly formal and poetic compared to what it really means in the Greek New Testament: "To weep or wail, with emphasis upon the noise accompanying the weeping."[3] Jesus didn't cry in a formal and poetic way. He cried the way we cry. Thus, those standing near conclude, "See how he loved him!" (v. 36).

Jesus' love for Lazarus is in Jesus' bones, guts, muscles, and tear ducts. Just as our love in us. This is why the early church so adamantly insisted that Jesus was a true human, not some kind of benevolent ghost. He is truly one of us. Jesus loves with his mind, spirit, and body. Jesus is with us in this world with a real body, in this world where death threatens us and doubt bothers us. We need not be ashamed to admit our doubt or fear to Jesus. If someone tries to bully us into thinking we're less than Christian when we feel

50

such things, they're advertising some small slice of truth, some sliver of Christian ideology; but, they're not facing the Bible's broader message that *even after Jesus' resurrection* his disciples more than once doubted him.

When I consider Jesus' genuinely human way of dealing with grief, I think of the little girl who ran to her mother, "Mommy! Mommy! Can I go to Crissy's house? She phoned and she's really upset. She lost her doll and she's been looking for it all morning."

Her mother said, "You think you can help her find it?"

"No," the little girl said, "but I can help her cry."

Jesus comes as a person who cares enough to sit next to you and cry, which is, sometimes, all we need. If we want a fix to all our problems, we can buy the newest self-help book that promises to fix us. We can send money to the TV evangelist who promises to fix us. Jesus, however, loves us no matter what — no matter how much money or how much faith we have. And most of the time love is enough.

John Templeton died July 8, 2008. He started the Templeton Growth Fund and gave his money to The Templeton Prize for religion, which grants a winner every year over a million dollars. "The Templeton Prize honors a living person who has made an exceptional contribution to affirming life's spiritual dimension, whether through insight, discovery, or practical works."[4] John Templeton was a lifelong Presbyterian. He believed that spiritual things are more important, finally, than material ones — even more important than the stock market, where he made his money. He realized that love is stronger than anything in this world. So, he provided funds for founding the Institute for Research on Unlimited Love. The purpose of the institute is bound to the belief that "[t]he essence of love is to affectively affirm as well as to unselfishly delight in the well-being of others, and to engage in acts of care and service on their behalf…"[5] That's a fairly good description of Jesus' love. And love, even research shows, is almost all we need, even when facing death.

I read about a man who for his dying wife put on her makeup every morning. She'd been able to put on her own makeup during the early stages of her illness. The woman was concerned with her appearance and so, as she grew weaker, her husband began to help her, until finally, although clumsily, he did it for her. Even when she was in a coma her husband still combed her hair and put on her lipstick and eyeliner. He didn't do a good job, but a loving one.[6]

When we face death, we bring our questions about God and faith; yet, if we are too frightened or numbed by death to ask questions, Jesus loves us enough to ask us questions. He says to Martha, "Those who believe in me, even though they die, will live, and everyone who lives and believes in me will never die. Do you believe this?" (vv. 25-26). Jesus cares for us so much that he helps us consider our faith. It can be hard to hold to faith in God, especially as we walk closer to the grave of a loved one or to a loved one hovering ever nearer death. But Jesus doesn't scold Mary or Martha or us because we think he hasn't been around at the right time. He loves us anyway. He loves us despite our doubt or our faith. He loves us all the way through life and through death and into our final life in the fullest presence of God. So it's one who loves us who asks, "Do you believe this?"

When we're shaky or when we're steady, we place our trust in Jesus who loves us. When we're thinking clearly or we're so muddled that friends insist someone else drive us, we trust, however imperfectly, Jesus who loves us.

Because Jesus shows us his unlimited love by what he says and by what he does, we believers don't view life and death the same as others. We now set out to be the loving presence for others that Jesus is for us; because, for us Jesus is life. Jesus is the resurrection and the life, meaning he's the source, explanation, and goal of life. Because Jesus loves us, we trust that our life isn't a mere tick in the clock of the cosmos. Because Jesus loves us, our life isn't a blink in the eye of eternity. Therefore because Jesus loves us, our death isn't a snowflake melting into the ocean of time. As we approach our end of the cemetery we trust Jesus that death isn't our brief light crashing into darkness. It's putting out our earthly lamp because God's true dawn has arrived.

Communion

To show how much God loves us, God sent Jesus as a genuine human, able to understand our doubts, feel our pain, and share our problems. We can trust Jesus' genuine concern for us throughout our living and all the way through our dying. Thus we also trust his invitation here — to come and receive the means of grace. Amen.

---

1. Johannes P. Louw and Eugene A. Nida, *Greek-English Lexicon of the New Testament Based on Semantic Domains* (New York: United Bible Societies, 1988), v. 1, p. 295.
2. Louw and Nida, p. 315.
3. Louw and Nida, p. 304.
4. www.templetonprize.org.
5. www.unlimitedloveinstitute.org.
6. Carolyn Burns in Patricia Anderson, *All of Us: Americans Talk about the Meaning of Death* (New York: Delacorte Press, 1996), pp. 233-234.

Remembering Jesus

The novel *The Ugly American* is based upon facts of how Americans related to people in Southeast Asia. The insensitivity and arrogance of American government officials was generally depressing. One chapter of the novel, however, is particularly inspiring. An American woman, Emma Atkins, has come with her engineer husband to the fictional nation of Sarkhan. Emma is a curious, good-hearted person and she soon notices that in their small village all the older people are permanently bent over.

She struggles with the language in order to ask neighbors why old people in the village are stooped. No one can answer. For her fellow villagers it's natural that old people are bent over, always have been. But Emma assumes there's a reason that every person over sixty is bent in a constant stoop. By the time the rainy season passes, she's set to delve into the cause of the old peoples' painful posture.

The monsoons end, people spend more time outdoors, and Emma realizes that village clean up is accomplished exclusively by the older people. Each day they sweep the ground with a broom made of palm fronds, yet the broom handle is only a couple feet long. The elderly spend their twilight years bent under a burden of their own making: the tradition of a short handled broom.

Emma talks with an old woman who is bent and crippled and tells her that sweeping bent over all day molds an older person into a permanent stoop. She suggests attaching a longer handle to the broom so people can stand upright while sweeping. The woman argues otherwise. Brooms always have short handles.

The reason, Emma discovers, is that wood is scarce in their area and putting a longer wood handle on a broom would seem a waste. Emma is creative and she's interested in helping people. She finds a reed plant that grows near and it has one strong central stock large enough to be a broom handle. She has her husband dig the reed plant out, cart it home, and plant it by their hut. The villagers are curious. Then one day when several of her neighbors are present, she cuts the central reed, binds it to the broom's fronds, and begins sweeping while standing upright. For a few days everyone watches her, then someone asks where she found a reed long enough for such a broom handle.

Emma and her husband soon move to work in another village and four years later, living again in the United States, a letter arrives from the village headman to Emma. He thanks her for demonstrating a new way to sweep and consequently unbending the backs of the village old people. The headman writes, "I know you are not of our religion, wife of the engineer, but perhaps you will be pleased to know that on the outskirts of our village we have constructed a small shrine in your memory. It is a simple affair; at the foot of the altar are these words: 'In memory of the woman who unbent the backs of our people.' And in front of the shrine there is a stack of the old short reeds that we used to use."[1]

Some people think the Bible always tells us what to do. Yet, read the Bible and you find that a great deal of the Bible shows us, which is a much more "telling" way to communicate: like Emma just sweeping away with her long-handled broom. Since we weren't alive in first-century Galilee and Judea, God has given us the gospel stories of Jesus so we too can see a divine way of living. Jesus isn't just a wonderful example, because try as we may we'll never live up to it. The Bible's four gospels are portraits, each from its own perspective, of how God lives among us. Our reading the gospels or hearing them read helps us see and remember

God's unique person and how he portrays divine life for us. Therefore, our first and most important task as Christians is to remember what we hear about Jesus.

A distinct and usable memory along with imagination sets us apart from the animal world. Animals remember, but humans can select our memories, find order and patterns in life, ponder experience, and learn. The philosopher Soren Kierkegaard stated, "Life must be lived forward, but it can only be understood backward." A good deal of our understanding life comes from using our memory.

In the Old Testament, when a person is commanded by God to remember, it means to bring something actively into the present and to let that memory lead us into appropriate behavior. The Old Testament demonstrates the active sense of memory in 1 Samuel. It tells of Hannah's being promised a child. The scripture says Elkanah knew his wife Hannah, which means they had sexual intercourse, and "the Lord remembered her. In due time Hannah conceived and bore a son" (1 Samuel 1:19-20). It's not as though God had forgotten Hannah; but, the whole sense of remembering in the Bible means to become active in doing something.

In fact, in the language of the Old Testament when one puts the verb "to remember" into the causal tense the meaning soars high beyond "to recall" until it means "to praise, extol, worship."[2] When we truly remember what God has done for us, our most authentic response as humans is to worship God. The same applies to such things as the commandment, "Remember the sabbath day, and keep it holy." To remember the sabbath doesn't mean just calling it to mind, but to observe it, to guard it, and to celebrate all that it means of God's grace to us. To remember Jesus means to bring him into our living.

"Remember," the Bible so often states. Our responsibility within the faith makes us attentive to our memory and we learn to regulate it, train it, use it. Because we can forget things. Ever stop in the kitchen and say, "Now, what was I here after?" That's known as "pondering the hereafter." Or you walk from the supermarket into the parking lot and say, "Where did I park?" It could be worse. You could stand there asking, "What kind of car do I own?"

Paul handed on the words of Jesus at his last supper in which Jesus specifically instructed his students to remember him. What were Jesus' students supposed to remember? That they never understood Jesus? That they tried to keep people away from him, people he wanted to see? That they struggled to be top of the group while he served them selflessly? Were they to remember that on Jesus' last night with them one of them betrayed him, one denied him three times, and all fled him?

What would Jesus have us remember about his last earthly meal with his students? Matthew reports for us: "While they were eating, Jesus took a loaf of bread, and after blessing it he broke it, gave it to the disciples, and said, 'Take, eat; this is my body.' Then he took a cup, and after giving thanks he gave it to them, saying, 'Drink from it, all of you; for this is my blood of the covenant, which is poured out for many for the forgiveness of sins' " (vv. 26-28).

Jesus' life, death, and this meal are "*for the forgiveness of sins.*" When we come to this meal, the bread and wine fill us with memories of Jesus. We feel solemn, because it's about his death. We're also joyful because we here share his resurrection. Some people plunge beyond solemn at communion. When they think about the sacrament of communion, they become stuck, because Jesus stated that what he did was for the forgiveness of *sins*. They obsess upon sins and miss forgiveness. From Jesus' point of view, our longer English word *forgiveness* is more important. Jesus forgives us. We get to start over with his resurrection, and we don't deserve it. His meal is about that. If we deserved it, it wouldn't be forgiveness. That's what we need to remember.

Yet our memory can malfunction. Our memory can ambush us, even in worship, even as we come to receive the means of grace in this bread and cup. Our memory can accuse us, "Did God really forgive that sin of yours? That was pretty awful, you know. Sure, God forgives others, but your sin was so stinking, so gigantic, so hurtful, with results that will leak into the lives of others and spread destruction through the coming generations. Where do you get off claiming forgiveness? You presume just to walk forward to this rail and be forgiven! *You*?"

A rotten memory can bother us. You could say that our memory misfires. Jesus, however, wants us to remember the forgiveness of sins. In the scriptures, in worship, and in this sacrament Jesus proclaims that the burden of sin is off us and onto him. His choice.

Again in the language of the Old Testament a word often used metaphorically for forgiveness literally means lifting up or carrying away.[3] When we truly remember Jesus, it sinks into us from our freed and forgiven memory that we've been lifted up to true life. The consequences of the meal Jesus serves remind us in miniature of what his entire life accomplished: Jesus lifts us up. Even if we are perpetually bent by arthritis or confined daily to a wheelchair, in the eyes of our Lord Jesus we stand before him as true human beings, heads lifted — not in arrogance, but looking now at the world as did Emma Atkins, in order to see where Jesus summons us to serve God by loving others.

Remember Jesus when you are doubtful. When you remember him, you'll find his very life activated in you again as his Spirit reaches and meets your spirit. Jesus loves us more than we expected and more than we deserve. I'm always taken by a radio talk show host who responds to the question, "How are you doing?" with the answer, "Better than I deserve." So it is with all of us, and we need to remember it.

Yet, we can forget God's grace to us and so we need to be reminded about what's really important, like the rich man who was marrying a much younger woman. In order to trust that she loved him more than his money, before they were married he had her promise that if he died first she'd bury his money with him. She agreed. A number of times in their marriage he asked her, "Do you remember you promised to bury my money with me?" She always said, "Yes." As he got older he reminded her more often and she always agreed. As expected he died before his wife and, sure enough, at his funeral she walked last to his open casket, reached in, and placed on his chest a check for three million dollars.

As Emma Atkins showed with her longer broom, sometimes we suffer because we can't imagine better ways to do things. At other times, as the rich man, we forget there are other ways to do things. So in worship we practice remembering Jesus and how he achieved lasting change for humanity. He loved us, even to death.

Along with our memories of the earthly Jesus we all bring our personal memories of experiences in which God's grace has reached us. I'm a bookish person, so no surprise that a special memory of mine is from a book. The book was about the faith of psychiatrists. One man related, "Undoubtedly the most important event of the year was 'falling in love' with Carola. February 15, 1934, when I first saw her at a concert, when I introduced myself (she already knew who I was), when I asked her if I could walk her home, when I ate her baking-powder biscuits, when I kissed her goodnight, was the memorable day in solving the question of my relationship with the opposite sex. I still occasionally buy her a rose on the fifteenth of the month — any month."[4]

"A memorable day" he said, a day he set out continually and joyfully to remember by doing something in response to the person he loved. We can do something to remember Jesus during any worship. We'll do what he commanded us here at this altar. But also, like the short brooms laid beside the altar in the fictional nation of Sarkhan, we can come today and lay down our dysfunctional ways of living that wear us out. Because Jesus forgives us, here we can drop our self-inflicted sins, the impediments that spiritually disable us and reduce us as human beings. We can continually and joyfully remember our Lord Jesus and realize that, as we serve him by loving others, he keeps lifting us up and up and up into the fullest stature of the children of God.

Communion

When we approach our Lord's table he commands us to remember. Recall here the grace of our Lord Jesus and let him again assure you that your sins, grievous as they seem to you, are forgiven. Leave here all things that prevent your living for Jesus and allow God's Holy Spirit to lead you now in forgiving others. Amen.

---

1. William J. Lederer and Eugene Burdick, *The Ugly American* (New York: Fawcett, 1958), pp. 196-201.
2. zcr
3. ns'
4. Donald F. Moore, "A Religious Autobiography," in Paul E. Johnson, *Healers of the Mind* (Nashville: Abingdon, 1972), p. 192.

Looking Down on God

One of the most interesting accounts of a creative and surprising story was of a father and his three-year-old daughter. During a long winter the little girl had enjoyed more and more using the sparse living room for her gymnasium and for the center of her imaginary world. All the room had in it was a large pillow. So the father set out to tell her a story about a pillow. He made up a story about a large pillow and a forest and animals that would come and play on the pillow. When all the animals slept, the pillow would go sleep with the clouds. Well, one night a huge wind blew away not only the clouds but the pillow too. The animals couldn't find the pillow. The father was about to finish the story, but the direction he was going doesn't make any difference; because, the daughter pointed and said, "And here it is, in our living room."[1]

So ended the story and ended it pretty well. That's a little of what happens when we read the stories in the Bible. We might think the Bible is about a time and place far away, maybe even a fanciful, float-in-the-air land that has nothing to do with us; but, with a thump the Bible story lands right here in this room where we gather for worship. Tonight the whole text from the Bible is transferred here — Jesus, Peter, Judas, and the entire crew.

Peter, always spokesman for the twelve, continues that function here. However, tonight he not only represents the other eleven, but us also. We'd do the same as he did. Jesus comes to wash our feet and we squirm away. When we talk about such lofty things as Jesus' loving us, that's fine; but, here he is shuffling over to us on his knees, not many clothes on either, and he's reaching to our feet with his hands. Has your teacher touched your feet lately? *Anybody* touch your feet lately? People hear the story of Jesus washing feet and leap to the conclusion that it's tough being a foot-washer. It certainly is. But, when the story drops out of the clouds and into this room, it includes us; we realize that for most of us, as for Peter, it's harder to have our feet washed than to wash others' feet.

If Jesus is going to come around and wash us, that makes us the powerless recipients of this embarrassing service. We might even suggest to Jesus, "How about if I carry the basin while you wash everyone else's feet? I can hand you dry towels. I'm more comfortable just helping out."

Jesus is insistent not only to Peter but to each of us who are hyperventilating as Jesus approaches. He insists that he has to do something for us that we can't do for ourselves, like set us right with God. Jesus says, "Unless I wash you, you have no share with me" (v. 8). Jesus has to do some basic things for us, and he knows what they are. We can't do them ourselves. It's Jesus' choice, also, how he does it.

What's really troubling is that Peter, feeling squeezed into this room with others and looking down on Jesus, is forced to view God from a strange perspective. He's already been getting God and Jesus mixed up. Now God's no longer high above Peter, but below, serving him. God serves us, which isn't the same as our wanting God to serve us, which we often do. We treat God like a servant, handing in our grocery list of prayer requests; but, when we stop to think carefully about God, our idea is a little more exalted. For Peter, getting his feet washed by God's representative on earth, smashes the picture he had of God. We can almost hear his former picture of God shattering into pieces on the floor next to Jesus' basin.

Here we are beside Peter, and Jesus is at our feet demonstrating God's basic nature: God serves. Jesus is satisfied and fulfilled by serving. It's who he is from the inside out. As we watch Jesus working his way down the row of his students coming always closer to us, we realize that service isn't a trivial thing for others to do, or for us to do selectively for those whom we think deserve it, or for us to do when others can appreciate it. Service is God's nature, and thus it's also God's true and original image upon us humans. Jesus says, "If I, your Lord and Teacher, have washed your feet, you also ought to wash one another's feet," (v. 14) which means doing even menial things if that's what others need.

Jesus goes so far as to define selfless service as the one proof by which people will know his followers. He looks up at us tonight, our foot in his hand, and states, "By this everyone will know that you are my disciples, if you have love for one another" (v. 35). For all the tests over the centuries that Christians have erected to determine who's a "real Christian," Jesus points only to one here — that we love one another as he loved us. Christians can pile up our requirements and qualifications for what people must do or believe before we consider them within God's grace. We can insist that they be baptized in a particular way or celebrate communion with a particular ritual, or that the church be governed in a specific way or by a particular sex, or that we bow to a precise theory of biblical inspiration or to a detailed schedule of how the world's going to end. Jesus grants one window through which the world can look in and spy the true church: Our loving one another.

Jesus says his commandment that we love one another is a new one. It's new in that love is now measured by Jesus' life. His love becomes the standard. "Just as I have loved you, you also should love one another" (v. 34). Christians are commanded to love Jesus' way, even if it includes a towel and a basin or a cross. Yet, we don't just imitate Jesus because we admire his example. Our emulation comes from more. Jesus loves us and his loving us is the greatest reason, the largest motive, the strongest incentive for us to love others. We love because we recognize he loved us. Gratitude is the deepest and most ethical of all emotions.

Alan Paton was a white South African who resisted apartheid. Because of what he said as he traveled and spoke outside of South Africa, the white South African government took away his passport for ten years. He was threatened and harassed, but he peacefully resisted the laws against human equality. He did so mostly by speaking and writing. One of his novels was *Ah, But Your Land Is Beautiful*. It's a historical novel set in South Africa in 1952-1958. Some characters in his novel are real. For other characters he uses real or typical events but changes names.

In the novel a black pastor invites a white South African judge to worship on Holy Thursday in a black church where they practice foot washing. The pastor hopes that the judge's attending will promote reconciliation and healing between races. The white judge is a good person, and he realizes he's taking a political risk to attend but he does attend. When it's time to wash feet, the judge is summoned forward to wash the feet of Martha Fortuin. She'd been a black servant in his house for thirty years. He kneels at her feet and realizes how tired she is. He understands that her weariness comes from serving him. He's overcome with emotion. He holds her feet in his hands and then — as she has held the feet of his children in her hands, washed them and then kissed them — he kisses her feet. People weep. The judge is motivated by his gratitude for Martha's service to his family more than he's motivated even by his deep sense of justice.

A white newspaper reporter happens to see this Acting Chief Justice enter the black church. The reporter has stepped in the back of the congregation, views the foot washing and the story spreads over all of South Africa's newspapers. The newspaper story ends the judge's political career. Sound a little like Judas in the room with Jesus?

Jesus points to the importance of his example when he says he's our teacher as well as our Lord. Notice first, however, that what Jesus does for his students is a genuine act of love. He's not just showing off. Martin Luther looked at ritual foot washing, where the king or pope or emperor washed the feet of a beggar and called it "ostentatious humility." Jesus' act of service was first genuine, not scripted, then Jesus noted it was typical of how he lived. Thus, Jesus' washing feet, because it summarized his entire lifestyle, becomes for us a symbol signifying much more. That night before his arrest Jesus' actions become a lens through which we see God. They demonstrate God's heart. Jesus' service is genuine to start with, thus it becomes a symbol full of more and more meaning that expands within the church and within each of us. Just like Jesus' cross — and all this occurring within worship.

In January 1996, in Waterville, Maine, a young mentally ill man who was off his medication forced his way into a Roman Catholic convent, killed two elderly nuns, and injured two others. That religious order and the town were traumatized. The nuns soon published a statement that they forgave the man. By then he was and still is in state custody. The nuns had immediately visited the young man's parents and shared their grief. However, when Holy Week came, the nuns decided they needed especially to help the young man's parents. They invited them to Holy Thursday's worship which included foot washing where they shared genuine concern and prayed for healing as they served one another in love.[2]

There the vast symbol of God's serving us when Jesus washed feet two millennia ago came back to earth in specific, genuine, suffering love for one another. Jesus was in their worship, serving, caring, re-creating the world, just as he did in the upper room and from the cross. Jesus is here in our worship. God still amazes us by bringing all the power and purpose of Jesus' last night with his students now right into this room.

Communion

When we come to this table in worship, God's grace leaps across eternity. Symbols expand here to new, personal, and challenging meaning. Jesus, typical of him, shows up at our feet serving us, whether we ask him to or not. His love and forgiveness meet us again in this room, whether in the basin and towel or in the bread and the cup. Amen.

---

1. William James O'Brien, *Stories to the Dark: Explorations in Religious Imagination* (New York: Paulist Press, 1977), pp. 8-9.
2. www.npr.org/templates/story/story.php?storyId=97092716.

Good Friday
John 18:1—19:42

Suffered under (Saint) Pontius Pilate

Christians Sunday by Sunday announce our collective memory of Pontius Pilate: "Suffered under Pontius Pilate." By repeating this creed regularly, we agree with church tradition and we don't wonder further about Pilate. We certainly have no sympathy for him.

Pilate's Jewish contemporaries had nothing good to say about him. Christians, especially on Good Friday, don't let anyone forget our opinion of him. However, some early church traditions decided that Pilate was a believer and two churches still, Ethiopic and Coptic, consider him a saint.

On Good Friday we always concentrate upon Jesus. For once, let's also spend a little time looking at Pilate. Officially in first-century Judea Pilate represents the Roman Empire, which means he stands for the power of the military overlord; because, Rome has occupied Palestine since 63 BC. Only a few Judeans at Jesus' time consider the Roman presence a benefit. Romans wouldn't be anywhere unless for their own self-serving reasons, which sometimes take five, ten, or twenty years to manifest themselves. Rome wants what is euphemistically called "taxes," but which is really tribute from conquered and submissive nations. They lust for the resources of their conquered provinces or at least use the province to buffer the Empire from enemies who might halt tax income. If the Roman Empire has a national anthem, it's "Keep That Tribute Coming." If people in Judea and Galilee don't believe this at Jesus' time, they'll find out during the first Jewish revolt 66-70 AD and the second 132-135.

Culturally Pilate is an outsider among these Jews, and he's far away from the real action of the empire. All the rumors, backroom conspiracies, and deals go on in Rome or in the officers' groups in Rome's larger armies. Here's Pilate, with his career languishing at the far corner of the empire, not a dream assignment and with few chances for advancement because he doesn't have a benefactor near to push him ahead in the world. And think of his wife. We can picture Pilate when he returned one afternoon to their pleasant Roman villa. He stepped in and announced, "Claudia, I've been posted to Judea." The least she would have said was, "Are you crazy?" — which assumes she even knew where Judea was. She's now stuck on the eastern fringes of Rome's sea, a month's travel away from Rome's salons, gossip, and malls. How's she to know the latest fashions, let alone order them made? No wonder she has nightmares.

Spiritually Pilate is the same as other Romans, believing in many gods. Maybe he fears them a little, but he probably doesn't take them too seriously. Certainly he's amazed as well as frustrated with his Judean subjects who not only insist upon one God but rule out all others. Betting one's devotions upon the head of one god can be understood, even admired. But where do these Jews get off claiming there *is* only one? We could compare Pilate's faith that allows for many gods with the current, stringent, unofficial, universal belief upon American university campuses. On secular campuses the consistent conviction, held even by atheists, is that all religions are the same.

Having reviewed Pilate's background, we see the difficulty that awaits him in Jerusalem. He's come as usual in the early spring for crowd control during the Jewish festival of Unleavened Bread and Passover. Early one Friday morning a delegation of religious leaders disturbs him, maybe they even disrupt his sleep. They bring a troublemaker for Pilate's judgment. The locals have authority to deal with some offenses, but everyone knows that when they show up at Pilate's Jerusalem headquarters, the prisoner is charged with a capital crime.

Christians at least once a year recall Pilate's going outside to deal with the accusers and then back inside to question Jesus — back and forth in a dispute that seems senseless to him. He starts with scorn upon his face and it doesn't take long to become absolute contempt. His teeth clench more tightly; and, perhaps more than once as he shuttles between these people for whom he cares nothing, he mumbles, "I get so tired of these idiots."

What's he have to deal with here... Jesus whose name has been drifting through the ranks, especially noticed by centurions. Pilate isn't going to waste time with this disagreeable situation. He has taxes to collect. He gets right to it. Let's deal with this clown and heave him out of here. With ridicule dripping from his voice he asks, "Are you the King of the Jews?"

That should end the whole ugly problem. No one in his right mind would answer "yes," because that's a death sentence. But what happens? Jesus responds, "Do you ask this on your own, or did others tell you about me?" (v. 8:34). Jesus here matches one modern stereotype of Jews, which I can repeat because I'm part Jewish. A man was in a philosophical argument with a Jewish colleague. He finally said, "Why do you Jews always answer a question with a question?" The Jew answered, "Why not?" Receiving the same kind of answer, Pilate thinks, "Oh, no, a smart aleck holy man. Why can't this kind stay in the desert looking for burning bushes?"

See what he's facing: Outside wait these haughty Jewish leaders who, of course, can't enter a non-Jew's domicile or they'd become ritually defiled. Inside stands this wacky itinerant preacher who's now going to banter word games with him. Pilate lets his irritation out, "I am not a Jew, am I? Your own nation and the chief priests have handed you over to me. What have you done?" Jesus answered, "My kingdom is not from this world. If my kingdom were from this world, my followers would be fighting to keep me from being handed over to the Jews. But as it is, my kingdom is not from here" (8:35-36). If this interrogation isn't completely simple, it's simple enough so that Pilate can end it by returning to where he started. This should clinch it. He asks Jesus, "So you *are* a king?"

If Pilate can get a clear statement from Jesus that he *is* a king, the nails are as good as pounded in the Galilean's arms and legs. Pilate doesn't need a superior to grant permission to execute a pretender to royalty.

When it comes to Jesus being a king, we Americans are almost clueless about what it means. The whole idea is distant from us. We don't live in the common first-century culture of the Mediterranean world. We have our three branches of government. A king was all three. Everyone then knew by experience what a king was. In the modern US what king do we deal with? The king of rock and roll? Burger king? We have no firsthand experience of kings — or of lords, for that matter. Think of the drill instructor in boot camp. His every word is a command and the only proper response to him is, "Sir! Yes sir!" That's only slightly the authority of a king. This shocks lots of American Christians who think of Jesus more as a pal than a commander. Perhaps we need to recalculate our thinking about Jesus. Pilate wants to make sure Jesus isn't dangerous. Lots of time that's us too. Our attitude to God is, "Don't say anything that my pal wouldn't say to me. My pal wouldn't confront me or challenge me. Let Jesus stay just my pal."

Jesus won't settle for Pilate's or our definition of a leader. I always like the statement of the British statesman Lord Balfour who remarked in Parliament, "Gentlemen, I do not mind being contradicted, and I am unperturbed when I am attacked, but I confess I have slight misgivings when I hear myself being explained." Jesus, however strange it seems to Pilate, explains himself, "You say that I am a king. For this I was born, and for this I came into the world, to testify to the truth. Everyone who belongs to the truth listens to my voice" (8:37).

Here Pilate gets thoroughly bogged down. He just shakes his head, sneers and asks, "What is truth?" He's exasperated as well as convinced that Jesus is innocent. Although this fellow is daft, you don't need to be executing lunatics. John's gospel reports of Pilate, "After he had said this, he went out to the Jews again and told them, 'I find no case against him. But you have a custom that I release someone for you at the Passover. Do you want me to release for you the King of the Jews?' They shouted in reply, 'Not this man, but Barabbas!' Now Barabbas was a bandit" (8:38-40).

Maybe Pilate doesn't catch it, but notice how Jesus turns the conversation. He goes from talking of kingship to truth: "You say that I am a king. For this I was born, and for this I came into the world, to testify to the truth. Everyone who belongs to the truth listens to my voice" (8:37). This mystifies Pilate. So, Pilate just gives up and allows public opinion to pronounce the verdict against Jesus.

Pilate doesn't understand what Jesus says about truth, and it's foreign to our way of thinking also. Jesus and Pilate are speaking Greek, the common international language. Pilate doesn't have a Berlitz phrase book or Rosetta Stone recordings to polish his Aramaic. He and Jesus use the same Greek words, but whoa! the space between them. Pilate would understand better if he knew some Old Testament background for "truth." In the Old Testament "truth" meant something dependable, secure, firm, supportive, reliable. So when Jesus talks about those who belong to the truth it means those for whom Jesus is the source of their life and those who grant him their allegiance. Not quite what Pilate concluded.

Yes, Jesus rules people as king, in that his followers will do what he wants. But Jesus speaks of truth for *how* he influences us. The night before said to his students, "I am the way, and the truth, and the life. No one comes to the Father except through me" (John 14:6). For Jesus "truth" isn't some abstract standard. Truth is Jesus himself. Truth is the way Jesus deals with people and the way he takes us to God. Truth is a lived relationship with Jesus. Jesus' truth, different than a mere true statement, is Jesus' life: all that he says and does and especially how he treats others. For us to live in Jesus' truth means to love and serve God and others Jesus' way. No wonder Pilate can't grasp the meaning.

Over the centuries the Christian church has often traded mouthing true doctrines for living within Jesus' truth. We repeat the creed. We line up our correct beliefs in a row and assume we're in the truth. Today any guy who captures a microphone can, what's called, "spin" the truth. This person's group can fall into any manure pile of scandal; yet, give the spokesman a chance and he'll put a new interpretive frame around an event, rename what happened, and come out smelling like a rose. That's the spin that changes the truth. It's different for those who live within Jesus. Jesus' truth changes us. Jesus' truth makes us more like him.

Once we admit how hard Jesus' truth is for us to understand or to do, we become a little more sensitive to Pilate's dilemma with Jesus. Pilate isn't just a slum landlord on a national scale. He's a lot like us. We and Pilate are alike in what we want from a leader. Do we want a leader who'll die and who tells us we need to die to ourselves? Do we want a leader who'll command us to love our enemies? This is a real command, and he's talking about the enemies we hate with a passion. Yes, those enemies! Wouldn't we rather have a leader who gives us even more than a financial stimulus or better rates to refinance our house? How about a leader who'll represent our values and defend us from our enemies?

If we're going to have a king, how about one who'll put us on the top of the world's heap?

So much about Jesus is incomprehensible both to Pilate and to us. As opposed to a leader who'll get us all we want, a good way to think of Jesus is to reflect upon the village of Eyam (pronounced "eem") in Derbyshire, England. Pulitzer Prize winner Geraldine Brooks' novel *Year of Wonders: A Novel of the Plague* relates how the village of Eyam in the summer of 1665 was struck with the plague. The village had a population of 350. The village pastor, William Mompesson, convinced the villagers to quarantine themselves to prevent the plague from spreading throughout northern England.

People from nearby villages left food at the perimeter of Eyam. By November of the next year when the plague had ended, 260 of its 350 villagers had died — including the pastor's wife. Those villagers, knowing the risks, chose to live for others. They followed a leader who lived within the truth of Jesus Christ. It was hard, as was Jesus' life, but the truth of Jesus not only inspired the villagers, it changed them and strengthened them to live as Jesus did... and to die as Jesus did.

Think about Pilate and Jesus: Pilate serving Rome's power and a multitude of gods, Jesus serving one God and all people. If we don't fit in either of those categories, it could be that we just believe in what benefits us and serve ourselves. Pilate finally turns Jesus over to be killed and Jesus accepts it, sacrificing himself for others. When Pilate asks the Jewish leaders, "Do you want me to release for you the King of the Jews?" we can interpret it as meaning, "Do you want this kind of a king?"

It's about the most important question God could put to us. Do we want this kind of king? Good Friday insists that we ask this question. To answer honestly we could stop and ask ourselves first if we'd want a pastor who'd convince us to hole up and die for the sake of others we don't even know.

Now, let's go back and consider if we really want a leader like Jesus.

Maybe the Ethiopic and Coptic churches think of Pilate as a saint because through him we continue to hear the question, "Do you want this kind of king, one who sacrifices self for God and others and who will lead you to do the same?" From two millennia away who can tell if Pilate was innocent? He said he was. If Pilate is partly responsible for our finally living within the costly but secure and reliable truth of Jesus, he's not history's greatest slug after all.

Communion

Jesus meets us today in a world of competing claims that water down faith to the lowest common denominator. Here in this difficult world Jesus is truth. We learn Jesus' truth not only with our minds but with our obedient behavior. Let us acknowledge Jesus as our king and obey him now as we come to his table to become more like him. Amen.

Easter Day
John 20:1-18

Putting the World Back Together

It's too soon after the murder to mention the names of the people involved; so, the following names are changed. In a small town, Janice, a young grade school teacher, had tried to break off a dating relationship with a young man. The young man had serious mental illness. He shot and killed Janice; then committed suicide. Her parents, Jack and Maxine, were friends with the young man's parents. In the midst of their grief Jack and Maxine got in their car and drove to call on his parents. No matter the tragedies, they set out soon, much quicker than I'd be able to do, to try keeping the relationship intact between them and the young man's parents. Consider the effort of those grieving parents as trying to put part of a broken world back together. And, reflecting upon Jesus' crucifixion, consider God's raising Jesus from the dead as God's setting out to put the broken world back together.

We can't gloss over that Jesus' death was a great tragedy. We can't just show up Easter morning and bask in Jesus' resurrection without acknowledging how terrible was his crucifixion and the circumstances in this world that bring about such evil. Not acknowledging the tragedy of Jesus' death would be like not admitting that the shooting of Janice was a tragedy.

We don't attend worship expecting to face the world's most unpleasant realities, but we don't deny them here, either. We all know tragedies: some caused by people we hate or love or used to love, some caused by germs or body tissues whose cells multiply irregularly, or by chemically impaired decisions of drivers, and some due to nature's violent whims. Life is full of disasters that aren't deserved and sufferings that can't be explained. We could slide over Jesus' suffering death by stating the grand theological conclusion that Jesus' death was meant to happen. But when we begin our reasoning in that manner instead of ending there after acknowledging a world of mysterious pain, we smooth over the catastrophe of Jesus' death.

Jesus' death was a tragedy. His death should not have happened. Humans by any standard should not allow such a miscarriage of justice. However, and this is the Bible's grand proclamation, God is so loving and so powerful that God would use even the worst that humans could do in order to bring this world back together, and God did it quickly. Ever count days between Jesus' death and the tomb being found empty? So many times Jesus said he'd be raised on the third day or after three days. Jesus said, "For just as Jonah was three days and three nights in the belly of the sea monster, so for three days and three nights the Son of Man will be in the heart of the earth" (Matthew 12:40). Count the days. Jesus died Friday at 3 p.m. and he was raised at least before dawn on Sunday. That's right. Not even two days.

I'll give you two explanations for this shortness of time. First is the scholarly explanation that Hebrews counted part of a day as a day. But the explanation I'm drawn to is that, considering all the evidence of the Bible, God couldn't wait to put the world back together. Think for a few minutes about Jesus' resurrection as God's hurrying to put the world back together. Things had gone so terribly wrong. God *hadn't* wanted Jesus to die. God wanted people to repent and believe in Jesus. If not, when Jesus preached, his telling people to repent and believe was some kind of pretense, a going through the motions because it wouldn't make any difference if or how many people repented and believed.

However one might reason about God's actions in Jesus' death, after God's chosen Messiah, God's unique Son was rejected and killed, God now set out as fast as possible to bring the world right again. We find out about it like this: Mary of Magdala walks outside the walls of old Jerusalem in the dark. It's dark in more ways than one. She starts to the tomb as the sky turns pink. Picture in your mind Mary approaching Jesus' tomb while it's quite dark, stumbling down the path through the unlit, ancient world. Mary hasn't slept for two nights, numbed by grief and still in shock. She should carefully watch every step but she can hardly manage a shuffle.

She saw Jesus die and John's gospel offers nothing that would have us conclude that Mary hopes Jesus is alive again. Why is she coming to the tomb now? Ask her and she probably can't even answer. She isn't coming because she's not thinking well, or thinking at all. We've all had times like that, when the mind doesn't work. Feet barely work. That's what disasters do to people.

When she realizes the rock that covered the tomb's door is moved, she dashes to tell Peter and Jesus' other student — probably has to wake them or finds them, also, sleepless. Especially we need to remember: After these men come to the tomb a total of three people have seen that Jesus is gone, but only one believes. The empty tomb doesn't prove Jesus has risen from the dead even for those who've been told ahead of time that Jesus would die and be raised. Beyond that, even when Jesus stands right beside Mary and asks, "Why are you weeping?" she doesn't believe in Jesus' resurrection. She only responds to the resurrected Jesus when he speaks her name. Mary comes here looking for a dead Jesus, but a resurrected Jesus has to find her and speak her name before she believes in him.

The gospel stories about Jesus' resurrection show that the news of his living again knocked people out of kilter. Read the resurrection accounts in the four gospels and see how they disagree on the details they relate — exactly as you'd expect when people live through the world's greatest event. Jesus' resurrection is exciting and disorienting. Its consequences echo through lives and centuries and can never be measured. As new as Jesus' resurrection was for the folk in Jerusalem two millennia ago, we already know the story. Most people attending church on Easter Sunday know about Jesus' resurrection. People might not believe it, but at least they know that the church for 2,000 years has proclaimed Jesus' resurrection. The church circles around and is held by Jesus' resurrection as surely as our planet orbits the sun. Jesus' resurrection is the center of the New Testament.

Nowadays, however, because we've heard it so much, the message of Jesus' resurrection sometimes receives a bored, wearisome, or skeptical response. Our continued Christian affirmation that the tomb was empty won't bring many people to faith, knowing that of the first three who physically saw the empty tomb, only one believed upon that evidence alone. Perhaps people would become more interested in Jesus' resurrection if they saw indications that it makes a difference in people's lives today. Nothing, even an empty tomb, is guaranteed to lead people to faith. Yet, we can at least turn our attention to modern-day demonstrations of God's putting the world right through Jesus' resurrection.

Looking at contemporary evidence of Jesus' living in Christians is complicated by modern attitudes. Today it's not just that people don't want to run to the empty tomb. It's not just that people don't want to put out the effort to bend down to look in the tomb. Many people today, if the truth of their hearts be told, are afraid that they'll get their hopes up only to have them smashed. It's happened to many of us — life's leading us to believe there's good reason to trust Christ and to rely upon his Spirit. Then we're slapped in the face by tragedy ripping our world apart, or by some ignorant preacher who seems to mention only hell, or by one of those well-known, old-fashioned, knock-down-drag-out church fights. We might have tried to believe once, but there's so much to sap our hope and to dump our faith like a wrecked truck spilling its load on the freeway. We might not look like it, but many of us come to Easter morning spiritually similar to Mary of Magdala, shuffling our feet wearily, merely walking forward in life and not even knowing why. For all the reasons not to believe, can we risk that Jesus' resurrection is really God's way to start putting life, our life, back together again?

Jacob Daniel DeShazer died March 15, 2008 in Salem, Oregon. He was 95 and most people remember him as one of Jimmy Doolittle's flyers who bombed Japan on April 18, 1942. That air strike was America's first offensive effort against the Empire of Japan after the Japanese sneak attack upon US forces at Pearl Harbor, Hawaii, December 7, 1941. DeShazer's crew bailed out over Japanese occupied territory in China. Some captured American airmen were executed. Jake was among those imprisoned for the rest of the war: 40 months, 36 months in solitary confinement. All the crewmen were beaten, tortured, and starved to near insanity. Jake hated his guards and all Japanese.

Then in May 1944, a guard delivered to Jake a Bible that the prisoners had received and were reading one by one. He had three weeks to keep it, during which he read it constantly and memorized much of it. On June 8, 1944, he accepted Christ as his Savior and Lord at which time he began to be flooded not only with the presence of God but with love for others, especially the Japanese. God met him there in prison, loved him, spoke to him, and summoned him to return to Japan after the war to spread the good news of God's love in Christ.

Two months after being released as a starved and abused prisoner of war he was in college in the United States. He completed four years of study in three in order to hurry back to Japan to announce the alternate existence that God offers in Jesus Christ. God forgives us so we'll forgive others. God

81

loves us so we'll love others. Jake spent thirty years speaking the good news of Jesus' resurrection. At one meeting in Japan Japanese soldiers attended who'd been his prison guards. They listened to Jake tell of the new world begun through Jesus and they committed themselves to the living Christ. God was hurrying through Jake DeShazer to put the world back together.

Jake wrote a pamphlet titled "I Was a Prisoner of Japan." Thirty million copies were printed and distributed not only in Japan, but around the world in twenty languages. A Japanese airman, Mitsuo Fuchida, was under subpoena to travel to Tokyo to testify in war crimes trials. He was terribly depressed and disillusioned. He'd believed in Japan and fought for his nation and yet Japan lost the war. As he got off the train in Tokyo an American man handed him a pamphlet. He put it in his pocket and later read of how Jake had been found by the resurrected Christ in a Japanese prison and how Jake now was sharing God's love with the Japanese. Mitsuo Fuchida then bought a book about Jake. Mitsuo Fuchida had been pondering some unexplainably gracious actions by other Christians in Japan. He wanted to know more about Christianity. He bought a Bible and put off reading it; but, when he started, he read every day in the foreign book and pondered its meaning. Slowly the story that seems old to us, maybe even boring because we've heard it all our lives, or so good we don't dare trust it, made a world of sense to him. When he read of Jesus' praying on the cross to forgive those who crucified him, Mitsuo Fuchida recognized Christ as his own Savior.

Within a few months Mitsuo Fuchida met Jake DeShazer and the two men spoke at large meetings in Japan to tell of the new life in Christ. Jake continued to speak all around Japan and Mitsuo Fuchida came to the US to speak. People listened intently to these two men talk about how God can put the world back together; because, the American man had been a Doolittle raider who had bombed Japan in April 1942, and the Japanese man had been the pilot in December 1941, who led 360 airplanes to bomb Pearl Harbor.[1]

What John wrote in his gospel and what Christians have said or done throughout history convinces only a few that Jesus is alive again and that through him God is hurrying to put the world back together. Just hearing what happened to Jake DeShazer and Mitsuo Fuchida and what they said and did might intrigue people but it won't lead many to trust Christ. Little can bring us to faith until we realize that Jesus, through all such things, is speaking to us, as he did to Mary that dark morning in the garden. We might not at first recognize the risen Jesus or perceive that he's speaking our name. We might mistake him for someone else. But that urging, that voice within us summoning us to faith, is the risen Jesus hurrying to heal what's broken in us and to put us back together. When we finally understand who's whispering our name in the depth of our soul, then we, too, hurry into God's world to help put it back together again.

Let us pray. Lord Jesus, no matter the dark or despair that might grip us, no matter the tragedies that have ambushed us, destroying family, friends, or national causes, this morning when we've been unsuccessful in finding you, we thank you for finding us. Speak our name in your life-giving, resurrected voice. Wipe away the skepticism or cynicism with which we defend ourselves against disappointment. Replace our doubt with certainty of your concern for us. Replace our hate with your love and help us forgive others as you have forgiven us so that we join you in putting your world back together again. In your name we pray. Amen.

Communion

As the risen Jesus spoke to Mary in the garden, so his Spirit speaks our name in worship. Our Lord Jesus knows our name, knows all about us, and loves us and forgives us anyway. He invites us now to his table from which he'll send us hurrying into God's world to help put it back together again. Amen.

---

1. C. Hoyt Watson, DeShazer (Coquitlam, B.C., Canada: Galaxy Communications, reprinted 1991). Gordon W. Prange, Donald M. Goldstein, and Katherine V. Dillon, *God's Samurai: Lead Pilot at Pearl Harbor* (Washington: Brassey's, 1990).

He's Back

Most Christians know about the Holy Spirit's power granted one morning in Jerusalem seven weeks after Jesus' resurrection. It occurred on the Jewish Festival of Passover recorded in Acts 2. Many Christians don't know what John 20 reports. This text is about Jesus' giving the Holy Spirit before the exciting spiritual event at the Passover Festival.

Seven weeks before Pentecost we're with Jesus late on the day of his resurrection. Jesus' resurrection has announced that he's back for good. His students thought he was gone forever. His enemies reckoned they'd safely stuffed him, dead, in a tomb. But his students' breathtaking (and breath-receiving) experience in John 20 shows that Jesus is back and will never again be absent from their lives.

We might as well get used to that with Jesus. He'll never truly leave us again. You assume that his death will end his influence in Jerusalem and pretty soon his followers are spreading his good news all over the eastern Mediterranean. You kill a few Christians in Roman arenas and before you know it Jesus' followers spread throughout the known world. You think you get Jesus stopped here, he pops up there. That's not only a summary of Christian history: That also is the pattern of our Christian experience until the end of days.

Remember when you were kids in a dozen different games of hiding and seeking, you always tried to double back and come up behind the other kids? That's what Jesus has done. He's circled around through suffering and death and returned. He'll always return. That's why we can't hold the

Bible casually as we read it. The scriptures tell us amazing things that are happening right now. Jesus is back.

As Jesus surprises his students on Sunday in John 20, so he does with us. He surprises us when we gather in worship with fellow believers. Who knows what Jesus will do here this morning? He surprises us when the Bible is read and when it's preached. Who can guess how his word will break into our lives? I was sitting in worship one day beside a woman. We said hello and shook hands during greeting. Then in the middle of the sermon she started hitting me with her bulletin: Whap! Whap! Whap! Surprise is one word that could describe my response. She saw a spider on me and she was dreadfully fearful of spiders. You know, it made me more aware of what might strike me during worship. One way or the other, Jesus circles around and comes back, especially on Sunday in worship.

As on that first Sunday, Jesus opens tombs sealed in despair and unlocks doors bolted in fear. He pries into the places we hide. The whole world lies exposed before him. We can only experience the world with the risen Jesus in it. He hasn't just slipped from his tomb. He doesn't merely pick locks in first-century Jerusalem. He opens all of life as easily as we crank open a can of chili con carne. Consequently, nothing and no one upon our planet is truly shut to Jesus. He's already here.

If you meet someone who has never gone to church or considered the Christian faith, don't be surprised if they mention that they've wondered about God or that they pray, even if they don't know to whom they pray. Jesus got to them before you did. Jesus is on the loose, from the morning of his resurrection until that evening that starts our text, and now beyond.

Jesus is smack in the middle of our life again. We can't keep him out. He obviously returns Sunday after Sunday. But he comes on weekdays too. So our house stands permanently accessible to Jesus. No matter what difficulties assault us from the outside or what fears grab us from the inside, Jesus is risen and we can't divest ourselves of him. We can ignore him, but we can't lock him out of our lives.

Jesus comes right through the walls, and that's not a comment upon the poor quality of buildings in first-century Jerusalem. Jesus appears suddenly and insists, whether or not he has an appointment, that we deal with him. We might think other things are more important: health, family, job, house, car, or vacation. We might even be concentrating upon improving our character or our church. Suddenly Jesus stands in front of us, eyeball to eyeball with us, and, when he speaks to us, it's about eternal matters. He tells us we'll never get away from him — that's what his resurrection is about.

In Jerusalem on that spring Sunday evening, Jesus' original students are locked in because they're frightened. Their fear keeps them even from leaving the house. They're paralyzed. We know what it's like to be stunned by grief, loss of a job, our beloved rejecting us, a war starting, an illness, or our crops or business failing. Yet Jesus roams the planet again, first in the shadows of resurrection morning and now in the shadows of that evening. Sunshine or shadow can't stop him. The tragedies in your life can't keep Jesus away from you, nor can all your worldly advantages. Jesus returns with unfinished business. He isn't done with you yet. He's just getting re-started.

Jesus doesn't meet with his dumbfounded students merely to restate the principles of his earthly ministry — that would mean nothing's changed. Jesus Christ our risen Lord is restarting creation. Jesus is raised on this *first* day of the week. The peace with which he greets his student is the peace that reigned upon God's very first day. If God's renewed creation wasn't obvious at that moment to Jesus' confused students, to the early Christians who later heard the gospel of John read in Greek, they'd instantly recognize the exact word — tense, voice, and mood — used of Jesus' granting the Holy Spirit to his students as God's blowing into Adam the first breath of life.[1]

After he's breathed on them and commanded them to receive the Holy Spirit, notice what Jesus tells his students, "If you forgive the sins of any, they are forgiven them" (v. 23). That's how Jesus starts the world over. It's also, if you consider your life in Jesus, how he starts over with each of us. The biggest problems in the world and in our lives aren't always caused by doubting as Thomas did, or by our sinning (Jesus dealt with that on the cross), but by our not forgiving. Jesus continues recreating the world by starting our forgiving others. Forgiving is what Jesus was about to the end of his natural life. Hanging on the cross he forgave; now, first day out of the tomb and he's telling us to do that also.

We assume religion is about forgiveness. We might not, personally, get around to forgiving, but we think religion in general is about forgiveness. At Jesus' time you'd expect Jesus after his resurrection to avenge his death. That's what others would've done. But Jesus forgives. He doesn't avenge his death and he won't let his followers try that either. Instead, Jesus sends us to live and act as he did. He dashes up to us like a runner in a relay race. He's not the last to carry the baton. He passes it to us, saying, "As the Father has sent me, so I send you" (v. 21). Jesus' suffering, death, and resurrection led to Jesus' sending us into the world with the energy of his message and with his same purpose of forgiving.

As we take off following Jesus, we can't live his kind of life without his Spirit within us. The tasks are too large and our responsibilities too grave, especially knowing that some won't believe that Jesus is alive again and offering eternal life. But the focus of our Christian lives, from the first day of re-creation, is that we are now Jesus' bearers of forgiveness and hope.

We find Jesus surprising us with hope when, having experienced discouragement, we continue trying to live for him for no reason we can identify in this natural world. It's supernatural — Jesus' Spirit making us hopeful, loving, and forgiving. Even when we don't see him around. Even when we don't feel his presence. It's just that he often wields his power in a hidden and quiet way. Jesus is invisibly roving the world and invisibly wandering inside us.

Jesus' Holy Spirit within us helps us know where Jesus is now, and what he's doing now, and where he's sending us now. Our worship and prayer conditions us to Jesus within us. So we practice praying. We regularly meditate upon scripture. We attend worship no matter what we feel like. Those are spiritual disciplines that open us to the grace God already has granted us through the Holy Spirit. The Holy Spirit's presence then helps us to see Jesus here; or, you can say to imagine Jesus, to see the image of Jesus here.

There's no place you can imagine where Jesus won't show up. So here's another spiritual discipline and we'll practice it now. I'd like you to close your eyes and *see* Jesus here in worship with us. Maybe he's standing across the room. Maybe he's sitting next to you but in your prayer see Jesus' image with us in worship….

Seeing Jesus clearly with prayer, thank him for what you're most grateful for….

Now, trusting that Jesus is always with you, in prayer bring to Jesus a person you need to forgive….

If it's difficult for you to forgive, watch Jesus approach you in worship, breathe upon you, and say, "Receive the Holy Spirit…."

Thank you, Jesus, for being with us, for appearing again in our lives, and for offering us grace to live on and a goal to live toward. Help us always to live within your presence and for your glory. Amen.

Please open your eyes.

The Bible doesn't just record Jesus' teaching but also tells us what he did so we can see him in first-century Palestine. Get used to seeing him in the Bible, and soon you start seeing him here; because, he's no longer entombed either in Jerusalem or in the first century. Jesus is here — the marks of the nails in his hands and the wound in his side.

Jesus shows up in the hopeless gloom of Easter morning and in the frightened apprehension of Easter evening and beyond. On Easter evening Jesus doesn't grant us the spiritual experience others enjoy a few weeks later on the Day of Pentecost. Yet Jesus gives us his Holy Spirit in order to bring his good news of forgiveness to others.

Jesus is our leader and one way to define a Christian is a person always trying to catch up with Jesus. Since Jesus is way out in front of us, we'd better get going after him and living his way; because, if we don't start following him now, he'll circle around and come back again and again until we do.

Communion

Our Lord Jesus has come back. He's risen from the dead and he's shown up again here in worship. As he served others before his resurrection, so by his present Holy Spirit he serves us at this table. Let us come here to receive the strength we need to follow him. Amen.

---

1. The Christians' first Bible wasn't the Hebrew Old Testament. Almost exclusively they read the Greek translation of the Hebrew, in which the verb, "he breathed upon" is exactly the same in the Greek of Genesis 2:7 and John 20:22.

On the Road with Jesus

Larry McMurtry's Pulitzer Prize-winning novel *Lonesome Dove* is about a cattle drive from Texas to Montana in about 1880. The novel includes the preparations for this 1,000-mile journey and a myriad of adventures along the way. A woman is taken on the drive: Lorena. This isn't just out of the ordinary. It's unique. She's brought along by a man who abandons her. She's then kidnapped and terribly abused by outlaws. Finally, Lorena is rescued and continues with the cattle drive, but she's deeply traumatized and defenseless, far from settlements, and she can only cling to the man who's rescued her and hope he'll continue to care for her.

That's all the romance and violence from the novel that we'll talk about this morning (all the stuff that gets our attention); because, next something more unexpected occurs. It's not violent or romantic, but more powerful. In Nebraska, Lorena is brought to a horse ranch and meets the owner, Clara, whose husband is dying. When these two women get to know one another the horse ranch owner, Clara, asks Lorena to stay and work with the family on the ranch. Lorena realizes almost instantly that she's offered a normal life. No matter how attached and hopeful she is about the man she's traveling with, Lorena chooses to stay. A genuinely compassionate and concerned person meets Lorena and she's not only rescued for a stable and respectable life, she's changed. Sometimes on life's road you meet someone who completely changes your life's direction.

The *Lonesome Dove* cattle drive helps us visualize life as a journey, a road on which we meet people and make decisions, and at times these people's questions help us make decisions. In the Bible it's easy to picture life as a journey. The Old Testament bursts with migrations, travels, and treks to freedom as well as to exile. It's full of sojourners and aliens who wander, and after the Exodus until the Hebrews become established in Canaan, they take a portable worship center on the road with them. In the Old Testament, journeys and caravans are such a constant occurrence that the word "road," which also means "path" or "way," takes on a figurative meaning of conduct or behavior. In the New Testament gospels you find constant traveling. Jesus is an itinerant preacher who depends on God's mercy and the charity of others to support his traveling. Within a generation after Jesus' resurrection the book of Acts records how joyful Christians journey throughout the Mediterranean basin with the good news.

This morning's text occurs just before the Christian faith fully explodes into the world. We're looking at the scripture's report of the first Easter afternoon. While in Jerusalem all is chaos among Jesus' followers, two of Jesus' students are on the road leading west from Jerusalem. Because they're leaving Jerusalem, we can assume they're giving up on Jesus. Their hopes for Jesus have been crushed. The man's dead! They abandon their journey of faith and head home to start over without him. We know there's more awaiting them on the journey, but they think they've reached the conclusion and at this point they've got every earthly reason to forsake their former direction. Maybe when they exited Jerusalem's gate, they even turned back with a gesture of disgust and said, "That's it. We're outta' here!"

Even though they don't know it, they're still on the road with Jesus. He just walks up and joins them but for the moment as the grammar of verse 16 implies,[1] God keeps them from recognizing Jesus. He asks them what they're discussing as they walk and they're astounded that he hasn't heard what's just occurred in Jerusalem. With Jesus' next question they go on and pour out their hearts, as airplane passengers often do when they discover they're sitting beside a pastor. Here's their great pain: They thought Jesus was the Messiah who'd form an army, toss out the Romans, and establish a free nation of Israel, and by the way, Israel would then dominate all other nations.

They're fleeing Jerusalem, but they've also been disturbed by a bunch of women. The women visited Jesus' tomb and discovered Jesus' body was gone. They returned to Jesus' other students, claiming that angels told them Jesus was alive. The women's report about an empty tomb was then confirmed by others, though they didn't see any angels. But these two ex-students know there's no way out of a crucified death.

At this point on their unknown walk with Jesus, he takes over and explains that the Old Testament aimed toward a Messiah who'd suffer. You could call this the "Genuine Jesus' Seminar," in case you've heard of the current "Jesus Seminar" that alleges nothing miraculous in the New Testament really occurred. This Genuine Jesus' Seminar is carried on walking away from Jerusalem with these sad ex-students. Maybe they too have given up belief in miracles.

As they continue their hike with Jesus, he leads them on a tour of the Old Testament. He shows that the pattern of the Old Testament is God's suffering both with and for Israel, and God's representatives suffer when they faithfully perform God's work. So Jesus isn't just the fulfillment of the Old Testament. His life's pattern is the key to how we understand the Old Testament. God keeps trying — even through suffering — to bring humans back to our created destiny within God's family. God keeps trying now, right here on the road with Jesus.

Jesus has taught a fine seminar on the Old Testament. He's interested these two fellows, no matter their broken hearts and muddled minds. But he's only intrigued them. If they were fish, we'd say they're hooked but not landed. Yet, Jesus' two disappointed, crestfallen ex-students demonstrate that they remember something of what the earthly Jesus taught them. They exercise hospitality and invite him to stay with them. The risen Jesus, no matter how his resurrected glory is hidden from their eyes, practices the same kind of ministry as the earthly Jesus: He goes in to eat with them. Before his resurrection he habitually ate with all kinds of people. No matter the Pharisees' strict religious regulations about whom and whom not to eat with, Jesus ate with everyone: rich, poor, religious, non-practicing, women, men, scoundrels, biblical scholars. He got into trouble for indiscriminately eating with people. Here he just continues what he's always done and eats with ex-believers who are hopeless, disillusioned, and confused.

While they're eating with this stranger who joined their gloomy journey, Jesus becomes the host and turns their meal into worship. "He took bread, blessed and broke it, and gave it to them. Then their eyes were opened, and they recognized him; and he vanished from their sight" (vv. 30-31). This is where Jesus' Old Testament summary comes alive, as though Jesus himself is a portable worship center. They realize that their hearts burned when Jesus walked with them and explained the Bible.

One can quote scripture all day and not impress people that it's any more important than the score of a baseball game. The objective statements of scripture must be confirmed by the subjective response of our heart. Boy do their hearts burn! And now also their eyes see. The two unfortunates have been on the road to understanding God's love. It's a suffering love, desiring that we all accept God's grace in Christ, and then that same love sends us out to *do* something about God's love.

These discouraged former believers have their faith re-ignited by Jesus. They return to Jerusalem, which they thought was the place of great disaster, but they find it the epicenter of Jesus' earthshaking resurrection. They rush to tell the others the news of what's happened on the road with Jesus and at the supper with Jesus. On the road and in the meal they've begun to understand what God can do even with human suffering.

That's the end of their story, and it's a happy ending. We should never, however, forget how painful was the beginning of their Easter evening walk. Jesus had suffered. We need to remember Jesus' meeting them in suffering because Jesus still joins us on life's real roads. He finds us in our pain, and even here he continues to teach us not only about the Bible, but about his resurrection's power in our lives. Jesus teaches us of God's love even when we think we've reached the end of life's road.

On August 31, 1983, in Anchorage, Alaska, Pam Joy Lowry got off the bus, unexpectedly darted in front of the bus into the street, was struck by a car and died. She was almost thirteen years old. Seventeen years later her mother, Christy, put in writing part of the family's experience in grieving for Pam. She published a little book, *Pam: Life Beyond Death; Joy Beyond Grief.* She told of the numbing grief as well as the friends, church, and pastor who helped her family and the special way that Pam's friends and their parents supported Pam's family as well as one another. Christy Lowry wrote of the family's visit to the morgue and the visits to the cemetery and how each member of the family grieved differently. Above all Christy affirmed that God was with them in that suffering. Christy had profound spiritual experiences that helped her to understand and to trust God's love even in grief.

As hard as it was to have one's child dead on the road, Christy dedicated her book for bereaved people "and their supporters as they journey together through loss toward a divinely intended, hard-won, and personal relationship with the Author of all of life."[2]

She calls grieving with God's help a "journey." Our Lord Jesus is alive and cares enough to join us on our journey, whether at the moment it's one of grief or joy. On life's road, he's the one we meet who's like none other. He'll walk with us and eat with us, teach us the Bible and host us at his table in worship. Even when we seem to be inviting him to come to us, we realize that he's inviting us to come to him, all of us who are weary and overburdened.

He comes to all kinds of people, those who are fresh out of hope or faith, those who are grieving, or those who are too shocked yet to grieve. And with the slightest response from us he'll take us with him forever.

Meeting Jesus changes us so that we now live for him and model our life upon him. Our task is to take Jesus with us into our homes and families, into our businesses and schools, into the neighborhood where people work and where children play and where tragedies and suffering occurs. This much we know about Jesus' style: If we won't take him to these places and to these people, he'll show up there anyway.

Communion

Our Lord Jesus is the host who invites us to this meal. He prepares the meal for those who are out of faith, out of hope, and out of love. He offers food to the disillusioned, confused, and doubting. We don't come here because we are abounding in virtue or goodness. We come because Jesus walks along life's road, finds us, and simply says, "Follow me." Amen.

---

1. The verb is in the passive voice, which I take as a "theological" or "divine" passive where the subject of the verb is not expressed, implying that God is the subject.
2. Christy Lowry, *Pam: Life Beyond Death; Joy Beyond Grief* (Anchorage: Christy Lowry, 2000), p. 10.

The Door of the Cross

Last summer my wife and I enjoyed visiting our friends Dick and Mary in Montana. They have about 45 quarter horses and they were thrilled to show us the herd and take us along one evening to feed them. That evening we also helped get a three-month-old filly into the barn in order to medicate a cut on her face. The filly was a little skittish, but we got her into the barn and into a large stall and then Dick tried to get a halter on her head to hold her still in order to clean and medicate the cut. She, however, would have none of it and even in the confinement of the stall was more than a handful.

Then a horse trainer friend of theirs popped in and asked if she could help. It took her about twenty minutes to calm the animal, and slowly she was able to clean its wound and to medicate it. She then led the quiet filly out of the stall and it returned to its mother.

Sometimes, even when we're trying to help, our way of leading doesn't work. Jesus in John 10 is explaining himself: Who he is and how *he* leads people. He doesn't talk about a quarter horse in the stall but about sheep into the sheepfold. The word for "sheepfold" in the original language of the New Testament basically means a courtyard, and thus any outside enclosure. Jesus says he doesn't wrestle or force people to God, but leads us there, and we know it's Jesus when he speaks to us.

Now, whenever someone tells you they've been hearing voices, unless they're talking about hearing neighbors through thin apartment walls, you need to worry. Hearing voices is almost always a sign of a mental health problem.

When Jesus says that his sheep know his voice, he means his followers can tell that Jesus is communicating with them. He says he calls us by name, which was very important in biblical times.

I grew up with a neighbor named Donna. Of all my childhood friends she's the only one whose middle name I know; because, when her mom was mad at her, she'd yell, "Donna *Marie!*" Sure, her mother knew her name! But in the biblical world one's name usually said something essential about you, who you really were. Jesus means that he knows our name in the best way, not to shout at us or threaten us, but to help us realize that he really knows us. He knows the true us that others don't know — like those things that shake us with fear. He knows our secret hopes that bubble within us, our painful regrets that nag our conscience, our deepest wounds that invisibly bleed, and our unfulfilled aspirations that still nudge us to be better than we are. He knows all such things about us and loves us anyway. Jesus, who knows us best, loves us most. We discern when Jesus speaks to us, because he wants what's best for us.

Darlene Deibler Rose had been a missionary in New Guinea for four years when the Imperial Japanese army and WWII ended her marriage and she began four years in a military prison. She endured incredible hardship and brutality, as did her other missionary associates, half of them dying. When the war ended, she was evacuated by ship to Seattle and was finally able to telephone her parents. We can understand how emotional that phone call was.

She later wrote about her faith in Christ and that first phone call in the US to her parents: "Many have asked me how I know it is the Lord speaking to me. What had just happened was the best illustration I know. I hadn't heard my mother's voice for over eight years, but when the receiver went up in Oakland, California, and I heard someone say, 'Hello, Darlene,' I knew it was Mother. No one ever spoke my name as she did. So it is, that when I hear deep within the recesses of my spirit someone say, 'My child,' I know it is my Lord. No one else calls me as he does. That is his promise to all his children.... The sheep hear his voice and he calls his own sheep by name, and leads them out."[1]

Even though later believers like Darlene Diebler Rose understand what Jesus meant, in his own time what he says doesn't make sense to the people he's talking to. Verse 6: "Jesus used this figure of speech with them, but they did not understand what he was saying to them." Jesus uses comparisons to explain how he cares for us and leads us. When it comes to talking about the heavenly realm, all we have are comparisons. Jesus uses these word pictures about himself in order to engage the minds of people at his time. So, living in a rural area, Jesus often talks about agriculture. Today, since few of us have sheep or a sheepfold behind the house, when we explain Jesus, we could make comparisons with machines, democracy, marketing, or computers, and always with the ways of human love. Yet, when we compare Jesus to anything, the comparison is always incomplete. No comparison to any fragment of this world is adequate to fully explain Jesus. And none of our comparisons can be literal. Think of it. Jesus says, "I am the vine. You are the branches." That doesn't mean that his skin feels like bark or his hair is green.

Jesus tries another comparison, "I am the gate for the sheep." Or, as older translations had it, "I am the door." The word "door" also means "gate, doorway, or gateway." Artists have a field day painting Jesus as the shepherd. But, how do you paint Jesus as a door? Easy enough to paint a gentle shepherd carrying a fragile lamb. A lot harder to show a gaping doorway or a swinging hunk of wood as a personal welcome to God.

The Santa Maria church sits on a hill in the city of Estepona, Spain. Two faces stare out from the arch over its beautifully carved main door: One face a male with his tongue sticking out at you and the other a female looking hopping mad. I photographed them and then printed those faces as postcards and sent them to my friends!

Maybe such artistry made some sense over a church door in 1772 when the place was built, but it's not exactly inviting today. When Jesus calls himself a door, he's not warning us or shooing us away from God. Jesus' naming himself the door is good news.

John le Carré writes spy novels in which you never know exactly what's true. In *The Little Drummer Girl* a daughter relates, supposedly, a description of her father after he's recently returned from prison and won't open doors. "He couldn't open them. He'd go up to them, stop, stand at attention with his feet together and his head down, and wait for the warder to come and unlock them...

"First time it happened, I couldn't believe it. I screamed at him. 'Open the bloody door!' His hand literally refused."[2]

For many people there seems a barrier as solid as a door between them and God; and, they won't face it, let alone move toward it. God and anything you say to portray God seems unwelcoming to them. That door seems forbidding. I'm a convert to the Christian faith. A few years into my ministry I heard the Sunday school ditty, "One door and only one and yet its sides are two. I'm on the inside, on which side are you?" I was livid. I know little kids and how they can taunt the outsider. I'd been outside the Christian faith. I could hear little kids singing that song and then see them stick their tongues out.

Jesus' calling himself the door isn't to frighten or belittle us, but to attract us. Our Lord Jesus is a completely open door, not one that only swings open with an arrogant, patronizing glee. And no one else controls that door.

In the middle ages when trade guilds passed on the knowledge of craftsmen, carpenters adopted the motto: "I am the door." When they made doors, they deliberately created the door's two small upper panels and the larger lower panels to form raised crosses. Most people have a door somewhere in the house with the sign of the cross on it. Think of Jesus' cross as a door that invites us to enter. As a way to be reminded of our Christian faith, we can remember Jesus' cross every time we open a door with a cross on it.

Jesus wants us to see him as an open door because he isn't a roadblock to God but an entryway. He's an open door to God's open heart. He not only shows us the way but *is* the way to God and the way to live for God. He's not an exit door out of life but in to true life, the kind we were created to live. Even Jesus' expression in verse 9 about allowing the sheep to come in and go out is an expression from the Old Testament that means moving about freely. The courtyard Jesus leads us into isn't a prison, but a temple. He brings us abundant life and true freedom, not cramped, half-way, someday-in-the-future life.

Sometimes the faith that the Bible tells us about is the faith to hang on to and endure. It's what I call the "getting-by-faith," as Darlene Diebler Rose clung to in a WWII Japanese military prison. Jesus tells us here in John 10 about a different aspect of faith. He's not offering us a faith so we can escape from life, as do some religions. He's also not granting a faith that always keeps us safe from the bad things in the world. Read the New Testament and see what happens to Jesus' closest followers!

Contrary to the popular understanding of eternal life, he's not only giving us long-lasting life. He promises, "I came that they may have life, and have it abundantly" (v. 10). Jesus changes the quality of our lives, not just the duration. The life he infuses within us helps us live in this world as he does — that's eternal, abundant life, and that's what's most important in this passage. Jesus' life here is "abundant."

Maybe our Sunday school teacher or some evangelist taught us to concentrate on getting to heaven; but Jesus didn't traipse around Galilee telling people, "think about getting into heaven." He told them to live within God's realm now, the God who's here right now in Jesus' invitation to life, who summons us through Jesus to live in a heavenly manner on earth. Jesus gives us that life now, more life than we expect or anticipate now, more than enough now. Also, by the way, we'll keep living beyond death. That's better news than just sometime after death being in heaven. Why wait? Jesus offers us life now.

Walter de la Mare's poem "The Listeners" pictures a horseman who's arrived at night and knocks on a door. The poem is mysterious as to who the horseman is and what's so important about his coming and knocking, but no one answers the door. Finally,

> he suddenly smote on the door, even
> Louder, and lifted his head:—
> "Tell them I came, and no one answer'd,
> That I kept my word," he said.
> Never the least stir made the listeners,
> Though every word he spake
> Fell echoing through the shadowiness of the still house
> From the one man left awake:
> Ay, they heard his foot upon the stirrup,
> And the sound of iron on stone,
> And how the silence surged softly backward,
> When the plunging hoofs were gone.[3]

Jesus' voice drifts through the door of the cross speaking our name. We don't have to fear him or fear when he comes and knocks at our door and summons us. He'll calm us with faith and strengthen us with hope. He'll lead us in love to true life here in the vast courtyard of God's creation. Eternal, abundant life starts here, trusting God and serving God joyfully as did our Lord Jesus whose entire life is pictured for us upon the open door of the cross.

Communion

Our Lord Jesus is the good shepherd who knows our name. He doesn't always lead us where we want to go, but where we need to go. Above all he leads us to the door of the cross, opens it, and invites us in to his true life. Let us now follow our Lord Jesus to his table and receive present evidence of abundant life. Amen.

---

1. Darlene Diebler Rose, *Evidence Not Seen* (San Francisco: Harper and Row, 1988), pp. 218-219.
2. John le Carré, *The Little Drummer Girl* (London: Hodder and Stoughton, 1984), p. 154.
3. Walter de la Mare, *Selected Poems* (New York: Holt, 1927), pp. 108-109.

Praying in Jesus' Name

It's good to be with you in worship. I appreciate the invitation to preach. I especially appreciate having a worship leader directing me around the chancel, because worship is done differently in different denominations — even within denominations. When you visit a different church, you don't always know what to expect. My wife and I visited here two years ago. I, ever eager to hear the sermon, chose to sit near the front, not realizing that no one would sit in front of us and you all know how you take communion here, but we didn't. Thankfully we received whispered instructions from the folk behind us. Maybe we didn't learn exactly how to receive communion with our Lutheran friends, but we *did* learn not to sit near the front when visiting a different church!

I heard about a visitor to worship in Kentucky who didn't know the local worship customs. Halfway into worship a boisterous child was hurried out, slung under the arm of his irate father. No one seemed to notice until the child cried out in a Southern accent, "Y'all pray for me now!"

Worship can be different. It can even be funny. I'm sure my prayers sometimes sound funny to God. It's okay to laugh in worship. It's okay to laugh in prayer. An especially helpful way for me to pray is to concentrate on God's grace and love entering my body with each breath in and my sin and bitter memories exiting from me as I breathe out. Do that right now. Breathe in and take in God's grace and forgiveness... Breathe out your sin and bitterness... In... Out... You can pray like this anytime, anywhere. However, it offers the double dangers of passing out either because you're holding your breath or hyperventilating. If you laugh while praying this way, it hurries up the prayer.

Our text in John 14 is about our life with God and prayer. We'll concentrate on what Jesus says here about prayer, starting with the most basic. First, to pray means to pray *with* God, and I emphasize "with" because prayer isn't just talking *to* God. God invites conversation with us by sending Jesus. God wants our attention, wants us to turn aside, leave what we're doing and whoever else we're talking to, and speak with God.

God wants to share our lives in prayer. Yet, our pious statements can demonstrate how we even leave God out of prayer. We say things like, "I believe in the power of prayer." That's like saying, "I believe in my wife's car. I believe in my wife's clothes. I believe in my wife's cooking." instead of "I believe in my wife." Saying we believe in the power of prayer can merely equate God with an automatic power switch. Yet prayer is even more than a conversation with a person, it's *living* with a person. Jesus speaks of heaven as God's house with many rooms for us, meaning that we live in the house with God. God is certainly more than a person, but God is at least a person. Therefore, I resist comparing God with television waves and saying that prayer is simply tuning in to what's already here; besides, most people have cable now. What does that do to the old comparison of God with television waves? We don't compare a person with electricity, although I've heard some people described as having the personality of a computer. Why should we say such things about God?

Prayer is speaking *with* God and not *about* God. We see and hear this while Jesus suffers on the cross. He cries out, "My God, my God, why have you forsaken me" (Matthew 27:46). No matter Jesus' pain or confusion, he directs his question to God. Sometimes our most honest prayers aren't when we're being all sweet and nice with God, using flowery phrases, but are those like Jesus' prayer from the cross — screaming to God in pain.

Since we're talking with God in prayer, I suggest we speak to God in conversational language as does the original Bible, although some ancient English translations of the Bible don't. The original Bible is in ordinary language, although the Hebrew in the book of Psalms tends to be more stilted. I've endured people praying in public, trying to use "thee's" and "thou's," and getting them all mixed up. Because God spoke to us in a common, human language we should at least begin speaking to God in the ordinary language of a child to a parent, not in an ancient English no one has spoken for centuries.

Jumbled "thee's" and "thou's" distract us who are listening to such a prayer; ultimately it's all right with God. If you can't pray any other way than with "thee's" and "thou's" go ahead. God wants you to pray, no matter how well you've mastered Elizabethan English or how poorly you've learned the grammar of your native language. I heard of a pastor who was greeted immediately after worship by a person who said, "This morning you made three grammatical mistakes in the pastoral prayer." To which the pastor responded, "That's okay. I wasn't talking to you." Our embarrassment with our language in prayer is unnecessary. If we're going to be embarrassed about anything in prayer, it should be our sin. That's what bothers God; yet, God forgives us and invites us not only to new life but summons us to prayer.

Whether our prayers are offered in formal solemnity or with stuttering uncertainty, prayer is talking with God. Prayer is conversing with someone who loves us infinitely. We don't pray because we're good, although we are good. Maybe the best reason to pray is because we're also bad. We don't pray because we have a lot to say that God doesn't know about. We pray because God loves us and wants to share our lives. That's part of our taking communion, sharing a meal at God's table.

A New York book editor arranged a meeting between author William Faulkner and physicist Albert Einstein. Despite the editor's efforts to get Faulkner to talk more, Faulkner remained mostly silent during the entire meeting. Later, the editor asked why Faulkner hadn't talked with Einstein. Faulkner said something like, "What could I mention to such a brilliant man that would have any significance?"

Some people feel that way about prayer, but God *wants* us to pray. God loves us. A sixteen-month-old child has nothing profound to tell its parents, but don't the parents hang on every word? Compare our praying to an infant's learning to talk. Praying is something we learn. It can be as slow as learning to speak a foreign language, even taking decades of daily hourly practice to begin to learn. But God wants us to learn.

A couple more suggestions for praying: faithful Christians have taught, "Not much speaking, but much prayer." You don't have to say a lot to pray. Start your prayer by reading a gospel: the record of Jesus' life and teaching. Gaze upon what Jesus does. Listen intently to what he says. Then imagine yourself there with him in that event. Ask Jesus a question or ask someone in the encounter with Jesus what's going on. Or just stand there in the middle of the event and watch and listen. If you don't think that's prayer, try it for half an hour a day and see what God tells you through scripture.

A second suggestion for prayer: Don't feel you can't mention details to God. A chronic modern belief is that God doesn't care about details. But life is only details. God already knows them. It's a sign that Christians aren't in touch with the God of the Bible if they insist on not praying specifically, by detail, for what really concerns them.

In my junior year of high school I had a friend named Doris. One night at a play we had a chat that got around to talking about God. I told her I wasn't sure about God. She told me five years after that conversation she prayed for me every day. I became a Christian a year and a half after our talk. Here in our worship we learn to pray for people specifically. God wants us to pray for individuals and for the congregation's individual ministries by name, and — as the text says — in the name of Jesus.

From the Bible our culture gets the saying, "in the name of." It's an idiom, an expression that isn't understandable word for word in another culture. We assume everyone everywhere understands that "in the name of" means on someone's behalf or with someone's authority. People in many cultures don't understand what "in the name of" means. I remember as a kid how strange it sounded in a western B movie when the posse said, "Open up in the name of the law," which meant they acted in a manner duly authorized by law.

Jesus offers a promise in today's text: "I will do whatever you ask…" But Jesus puts a condition on answering our prayer: "*If* in my name you ask me for anything, I will do it." Jesus assures us of his unconditional love, but he puts a condition on our prayers. We have a test for our prayer: Can we make our requests in Jesus' name, which means in his personality, in his character, in his spirit, or are we praying as Jesus would pray? Are our prayers only lobbying in the halls of heaven for personal interests? Or are they, as Jesus directed, "that the Father's glory will be shown through the Son?"

Praying in Jesus' name sifts our motives and lifts our sights and finally it allows us to hear God speak to us in prayer. Our reading scripture and listening in prayer gives God a chance to speak to us. An example of how God speaks to us in prayer is the early life of E. Stanley Jones, the great Methodist evangelist, missionary, and social reformer. He was speaking at Asbury College about the need for students to consider becoming missionaries. He prayed that God would give him one missionary as the result of his talk to the students. God answered his prayer by giving E. Stanley Jones himself a personal call to become a missionary. In a sense, E. Stanley Jones was the answer to his own prayer.

In the name of Jesus pray for this church and your pastor. Pastors pray for others. Pastors and their families need your prayers. When I was pastor in Klamath Falls, Oregon, the majority of the time in worship I didn't offer the long prayer, which Presbyterians call the "pastoral prayer." Members of the congregation did. When Dorothy Proctor offered that prayer, she always prayed for "our pastor and his family." Since pastors and pastors' spouses are used to praying for others and listening to the problems of others, to this day my emotions are tender by the memory of someone praying for us.

Pray specifically for your friends, relatives, neighbors, community, pastor, and congregation. Pray in the name of the Spirit and the character of Jesus because that's what God wants to give you in your life — the Holy Spirit of Jesus now risen from the dead and alive in you. Pray, watch, and wait for God to answer your prayer in Jesus' name. Maybe Jesus will answer your prayer by your living more of his life right here, right now. He promises, "I will do whatever you ask in my name, so that the Father may be glorified in the Son. If *in my name* you ask me for anything, I will do it" (vv. 13-14).

Communion

What do you do in worship as you wait for communion? I don't mean do you sit or stand or pass the elements. I mean in your soul. I suggest you pray, and that you do so by receiving God into your life with each breath in, and letting go of your sin and bitterness with each breath out. Receiving God in every breath prepares you to receive Jesus' body broken for you and his blood poured out for you.

If you just can't decide what to pray for as you wait to receive the elements of the Lord's Supper, trust what Paul writes in Romans 8. He says that in heaven the Holy Spirit prays for you. He says, also, that in heaven Jesus prays for you. So, if you can't decide what or how to pray, cast yourself on heaven's mercy and say, "Y'all pray for me now." Amen.

Easter 6
John 14:15-21

Duuuh!

If you've been around the Christian faith for a while, you've noticed how people pick what they like from the Bible. Like a giant magnet at a wrecking yard we each reach down into the material of the Bible and pick up only what we want — get the iron, leave the wood, paper, and plastics. We're not convincing if we say, "I don't do it but everyone else does." We all do. It's just that some are so obvious about it. I've dealt with two main types of Bible-selectors.

One brand of Christian Bible-selector is the person who snatches every word about love. In our text they hear Jesus say, "If you love me...." and they get misty-eyed, as they do about most of what's in the Bible, because they're convinced it's all about love. This person can see love in the Bible where love isn't around for 100 miles. But they'll add, subtract, multiply, or divide what the Bible says in order to wedge in some sentimental sense of love. For example, in today's text, they'll remember the old English translation for Jesus' Spirit, "The Comforter," by which they imagine something like the comforter on Grandma's featherbed. Although no translation can adequately render this one word, today's translation is much more accurate when it reads, "I will ask the Father, and he will give you another 'Advocate.' " By his Spirit Jesus doesn't promise a constant patting on the back, "There, there." That might be what we want, but Jesus offers us something else. Jesus grants us his Spirit to make us strong to live as he did. Contrary to our preference, God doesn't coddle us. God strengths us to live in our world as Jesus did in the first-century world.

Then there's the other large group of Christian Bible-selectors and these people don't latch onto the Bible's teaching about love. This group approaches the Bible and the Christian faith from an entirely different direction. No worry about their over-emphasizing love. They grimly clutch to our obligations and responsibilities. If some people get teary-eyed hearing Jesus say in verse 15, "If you love me," these others set their chins tight and recite the second half of the verse, "You will keep my commandments." There are fewer of this Christian breed, but they're out there, ready to point fingers at frivolous joy, wag their heads disapprovingly at human frailties, and especially frown at children who giggle in church. Give them a chance to talk about Christianity, and they'll pound on the word *duty* until any semblance of delight or any shade of happiness is beaten out of the Christian faith. They've never caught on that in the Bible God's laws are for our benefit.

Over twenty years ago I drove through Spencer, Nebraska, on Highway 281. The speed limit through the town was thirty miles an hour. However, the street was brick and had become something like a roller-coaster for cars. No one drove thirty miles an hour through town! The speed limit was to keep from hurting your car! That's like the graciousness of God's rules. God doesn't intend to abuse us with the Bible's commandments but to protect us from what life will do to us if we live otherwise.

No matter what parts of the Bible we most gravitate toward, Jesus, on the night he's betrayed, gives us all enough to occupy our feeling, thinking, and working for the rest of our lives. He says, "If you love me, you will keep my commandments" (v. 15). That's our full response to Jesus: loving him and keeping his commandments. Even though many of us like to emphasize one over the other, loving Jesus and keeping his commandments aren't mutually exclusive. Saint Augustine of Hippo stated this well in the early fifth century, "Here is the rule: Love, and do what you will." See how that works? If you truly love God and others, you should be able to figure out how to live.

Edward P. Jones' bestselling novel *The Known World* is mostly about blacks in the pre-Civil War south who own black slaves. Sounds strange but such things happened. In it Augustus works for years to buy himself from slavery. For more years Augustus works to buy his wife Mildred from slavery. Finally, after the father and mother's being separated from their son for years and able to see him at the most once a week, Augustus earns enough money to buy his grown son Henry from slavery. A critical scene later occurs when the young black man, Henry, announces to his parents that from his former master he has purchased a slave for himself.

As anyone would expect, his parents are furious with Henry. Henry doesn't understand, even though he's been a slave himself and his father has labored to buy his freedom that it's wrong to enslave others. The scene ends with the father's breaking Henry's shoulder with a walking stick and never talking to him again.

Having been freed from slavery, Henry should have figured out not to enslave another. More than the Christian religion teaches the Golden Rule: "Do unto others...." The Old Testament continually tells the Hebrews that because they were slaves and aliens in Egypt they should especially care for the slaves and aliens in Israel. We also, having been loved and freed by Christ, should be able to figure out how to love and obey him.

Jesus gives us what we need in order to do both. In John 14 he promises to grant us another Advocate, the Spirit of truth, so that through the Spirit we'll again encounter the living Jesus without his being present bodily. In order for us to grasp Jesus' immediate and intimate presence in his Spirit, consider this translation of Jesus' words, "I will ask the Father, and he will give you another Jesus." Catch that? "I will ask the Father, and he will give you another Jesus." We might want a comforter, but we get another Jesus. Remember, Jesus both loves us unconditionally and also makes impossible demands upon us. When you're God you get to do that.

Now that another Jesus is alive in this world, look where he is. Jesus says, "He will be in you" (v. 17). As amazing as it was for Jesus to be born through a virgin as a baby, it's equally amazing that Jesus is now born in us, taking human form in us, living in this world inside us. In theological terms, he's now incarnate in us, meaning that Jesus has taken on human flesh in us. Jesus was God's gift to the world, becoming incarnate through Mary. Now the Holy Spirit, the other Jesus, is born in our very lives — God's gift to the world through each of us.

For the last half of my life I've returned repeatedly to compare Jesus' Spirit within us to what a man told about his daughter. His daughter was adopted and she'd never known her biological parents. When this adopted daughter was grown and gave birth to her first child, she held the newborn infant in her arms. She said, "For the first time in my life, I'm touching my own flesh and blood." When we allow Jesus to be born into our lives *he*, with the eternity of God's longing to be with us, says, "You at last are my flesh and blood." Without Jesus we are cosmic orphans, separated from our original source of life. Jesus, however, promises in verse 18, "I will not leave you orphans."[1]

You can think of Jesus' family relationship with us in a couple of ways. You could consider us adopted as Jesus' brothers and sisters, as Paul the apostle does. Or you can consider that Jesus has entered into your life, into your flesh and blood, and that way you and he are now family. Whichever way we think of it, the consequences of our relationship to God through Jesus is that we now live Jesus' life on earth.

We're Jesus' family now, having received a whole new origin for our lives. We're not feral children raised by the world's wolves. We're no longer spiritually displaced people blown around in a whirlwind of competing loyalties. We're not lost as we flee dangers we can't even name, not floundering without a glimpse of an eternal destiny. We're God's family through Jesus Christ, and we can hold our head up wherever we are and whatever we're going through.

It won't all be fun. Jesus didn't always have fun. But we'll find that Jesus' Spirit within us will get us through whatever we face. He'll be with us. He promises he will abide with us, meaning he'll stick with us. If even our parents or children won't stick with us, Jesus will. We're in Jesus' heavenly family.

Jesus within us now gives us more and more of a family resemblance to our heavenly Father. Jesus within us helps us so we'll help others. He loves us so we'll love others. As Christians we're not free agents negotiating with God to squeeze out every benefit for ourselves. We're in God's family and we now do our best to get the good news of Jesus Christ to others. We tend to forget this. That's one reason we come to worship: to be reminded of how much we're loved and thus how much we need to get that love to others. It should be obvious. As John wrote in his first letter, "We love because he first loved us" (1 John 4:19). When we forget this, we need to hear the universal statement that is pronounced when someone doesn't understand the obvious. You remember it, I'm sure. When we forget that God loves us in order that we love others, a universal statement sounds forth, usually from a teenager. It goes, "Duuuh!"

We all have needs clamoring within us to get our attention; that's why Jesus' Spirit within us has to rap a little on us so we remember we're no longer in this life just for ourselves. When we don't quite remember what the Christian life is about, maybe Jesus who lives within us says, "Duuuh!"

He says, "If you love me, you will keep my commandments" (v. 15). As Augustine put it, we can love and do as we will. We should be able to work out the consequences of our being in Jesus' family. A woman who understood this, no matter how little money she had, wrote every month on the memo line of her check to the church, "In gratitude." She didn't need anyone to thump her on the head — or smash her shoulder — to understand how to live with Jesus within her.

Another individual who has grasped the deepest sense of loving as he was loved is a man who was in an auto accident and lost an arm. For the rest of his life he lays down his other arm and gives blood as regularly as he can. He received a number of units of blood after his accident. He doesn't need a long list of rules to guide him. He has grasped the full sense of gratitude for those who loved him with their blood. Nobody will say, "Duuuh" about his response to the grace that came to him from others.

It's obvious how we should live. Jesus gave his lifeblood for us. We're now his flesh and blood on earth as he dwells within us. Even if we're disabled physically or poor in the world's standards, since Jesus is within us it's now our nature, our own flesh and blood, to live for him. It's unnatural and unreasonable to do otherwise, because if we love Jesus we will keep his commandments.

Communion

By Jesus dwelling within us he again takes on human flesh and blood, and he provides for us regularly to receive his flesh and blood when we come to his table. Remembering how much Jesus loves us, may this meal help us live as he would in our world. Amen.

1. Although the NRSV translates verse 18, "I will not leave you orphaned," it's also possible to translate, "I will not leave you orphans."

Ascension of Our Lord
Luke 24:44-53

He Ascended into Heaven

After John Glenn was the first American astronaut to orbit the earth, he met with the Soviet astronaut Titov. The Russian asked him sarcastically if he had somehow met God in his spaceflight. Glenn responded that he believed in a God that you couldn't see from the window of a space capsule. And so John Glenn spoke for modern Christians, because when you consider what Christians have believed about God for 2,000 years, the idea that you'd go up in the air and *not* see God is a modern idea indeed.

In the Bible people didn't believe the world was round. Our ancestors of faith didn't perceive that planets orbit the sun. They didn't know about the speed of light, black holes, quarks, super novas, and other such modern discoveries. They thought of the physical universe in three layers: Below us was the world of the dead — in Hebrew it was named *Sheol*, in Greek *Hades*. Then the earth that we walk on here, and heaven was above the lower surface of the sky. A few smart Greeks knew that the world was round, but other people in the ancient world viewed the earth much the same as the people in the Bible.

In terms of the long history of the Christian faith, Christians have only recently been shocked to realize that the earth isn't the center of all those sparkling lights in the night sky. Many people even lost their faith when they realized that this world where Abraham and Sarah dwelled and where Jesus' cross was raised seemed transplanted from dead center of all existence to a minor role in an out of the way universe on the edge of a galaxy, which itself is but a snowflake in a cosmic blizzard.

It was a fundamental reorienting of thought and life to picture our earth spinning in space as an unimportant speck amid billions of larger bodies. And this complete turning around of our thought occurs now in each of us as we grow up. Every child begins by picturing heaven as up and usually we also picture God as a bearded old man sitting on a throne. It's nearly impossible for young children to think of God not having a body and heaven not being up. If you've been raised in the traditional language of the Apostles' Creed, you understand the little boy's explanation for why there's evil continuing in the world even after Jesus. He said that since Jesus ascended to heaven, God's been pinned down because Jesus has been sitting on God's right hand.

Most of us mature beyond thinking of heaven only as up or God only as an elderly male. The Bible encourages us to do so. As Luke writes, Jesus "opened their minds to understand the scriptures" (v. 45). Specifically Jesus was talking about the Old Testament's pointing to a Messiah who suffered — this is different than what was expected. Generally, we realize that the Bible doesn't always mean what little we first thought it meant. Fortunately, because God loves us, God deals with us in ways we understand. God meets us in a manner we can grasp, with truth framed in words and concepts people can wrap their minds around. For first-century Christians it isn't surprising that God took Jesus "up" to heaven, because it's natural for humans to think of God as up.

Many of our family have explored the pyramids in Mexico. I've heard people say that Egyptians must have sailed to America and taught Central Americans how to construct pyramids or that spacemen landed in both places and taught everybody. They don't consider that people from time immemorial have climbed to the top of hills to worship. Just as no one had to teach each religion around the world to use water in cleaning ceremonies, so no one has to teach us "up" as a direction to worship, even if we have to build pyramids as artificial mountains. It's born within our species and implanted deeply in our subconscious: "Up" is toward God.

Yet, we come to Jesus' ascension as modern folk, admitting that we can't get to heaven by climbing a ladder. Because we know more about the physical universe than the ancient folk, we're responsible to think deeper about Jesus' ascension to determine the further meaning it holds for Christians.

First, our English language helps us distinguish between "sky" and "heaven." The Hebrew of the Old Testament and the Greek of the New Testament each had only one word for both "sky" and "heaven"; fortunately, our language helps us separate the physical from the spiritual.

Second, as we meditate upon Jesus' ascension (as well as upon his resurrection) we're better off than Christians who were bombarded by popular scientific theories in the first half of the twentieth century. They were enthralled by what's now called the "old science." After 1950, humans have created new atoms and understand better the moment by moment creation and destruction of atoms in the sun. Today many scientists — not all, but many — have become more humble about the spiritual possibilities in this physical world.

In many ways it's easier for people after 1950 to consider Jesus' resurrection and ascension, because we can conceptualize matter and energy trading places. Christians now postulate all kinds of scientifically plausible theories about Jesus' body physically returning to God from a hillock east of Jerusalem. Some of those theories are sophisticated applications of $E=MC^2$ and others are more humorous: about Jesus blasting off toward the sky by the energy of a star-particle powered jet pack. Yet a lot of ordinary Christians remain stuck in an old science that thought it held the physical world tightly, believing that existence is closed to outside influence, and if it's not scientifically explainable it's not real.

Not only physical scientists, but plenty of medical workers have experiences that point to a physical world that's quite open to the spiritual realm. Dr. Lori Wiener serves in the National Cancer Institute of Maryland. She's a social worker and coordinator of the Pediatric HIV Psychosocial Support Program. She's dealt with many children who claim they've been visited and comforted by children who've died of AIDS. Wiener tells of one child who was having lunch with her mother and looked up, waved, and said, "Bye-bye, Allen. Bye-bye." The mother asked what she was talking about. The daughter said he was saying good-bye to Allen because he was now with Jesus. The mother assured her Allen was fine. Less than half an hour later a phone call reported Allen had died.[1]

We could debate if, how, and why Jesus' body physically ascended. The best way to profit from this text, however, is to look at how Jesus leaves his disciples. The last thing he does is to lift his hands and bless them. He's calling God's favor upon them, granting them God's presence, since Jesus won't be physically present with them again.

The apostles aren't sad. Think of the children you see at the county fair who lose the grip on their helium balloon and, as it floats away, they weep. Of course they don't cry long. Last event like this I saw, the kid turned to the parent, started pounding with his fist and saying, "Buy me another one. Buy me another one." It's not like that with Jesus' apostles. They don't feel abandoned. They hurry off to Jerusalem's temple to give thanks to God. Under Jesus' blessing hands this small group of Christians who see Jesus ascend to heaven is the nucleus of God's worshiping church, a nucleus as strong and powerful as the nucleus of any atom.

The last thing Jesus does is raise his hands to bless his followers and the last thing he says is a promise: "And see,

I am sending upon you what my Father promised; so stay here in the city until you have been clothed with power from on high" (v. 49). In the gospel of Luke those are Jesus' last words on earth. Jesus promises that God has more for us. God will do something that will finally bring us to solid faith and send us out into selfless ministry. Think of what it's like for those apostles. The resurrected Jesus as much as says to them, "You thought that facing a dead person come back to life was overpowering? Wait until the very presence and power of God dwells within you. Stay here, wait, think, pray, prepare, because the miracle of my resurrection will extend to you." The risen Jesus will come around you, over and under you, and within you. That's a promise.

Notice that these first Christians don't go back to the Mount of Olives every day to reminisce about seeing Jesus ascend beyond their sight. When the apostle Paul finally visits Jerusalem after becoming a Christian outside Judea and then traveling years as a missionary, he doesn't rush up to Jerusalem's Christians and say, "Let me see where Jesus ascended to heaven." He also doesn't say, "Show me Jesus' empty tomb." Those first Christians have the internal evidence of the Holy Spirit that Jesus is still with them, knowing their pains and problems, their hopes and joys. Jesus is with them in failure and success, in anxiety and ecstasy. That's why they gather for worship.

And so it is with us. Jesus' ascension means that Jesus with God is directing our Christian life from the invisible spiritual realm we call heaven. Jesus isn't gone from earth, but released from the physical constraints of living in one place at a time. I think of Jesus like the mother with nine kids who said she tried to be everywhere at once. Maybe that's been your experience as a mother. Because of Jesus' ascension, he really is everywhere at once, everywhere that people are in need, everywhere that justice is denied, and everywhere people struggle to believe. That's our basic faith as we worship: Jesus is here. Jesus is present and concerned about how we vote and spend our money, how we treat our spouses, children, and neighbors. Jesus is involved in how and where we volunteer and where we work, where we suffer and where we serve. Whether we live or whether we die, everything is under Jesus' blessing and power.

Jesus promises that the Holy Spirit will clothe us. When God encloses you into this very energy of heaven, you are able to live for Jesus on earth. You find that the boundary between the physical and the spiritual realm is what scientists call a "semi-permeable" membrane. Your life isn't closed to God's presence. God constantly opens you to heaven's influence.

We experience Jesus' presence different ways. We need to be clear about that. Some Christians think we should have a cookie-cutter experience of Jesus. Jesus, however, because he loves us all the same, distributes different gifts to us. We don't always share our experience, but we do share our Lord. I will suggest only a few ways I know that Jesus is experienced. You experience Jesus now when you're laid off, yet you begin to feel free; when you've been given a fatal diagnosis, and are surprised that along with fear you find peace; when you see the spouse who divorced you and left you for another, yet you feel pity instead of malice; when the yearly request for the church pledge comes and you increase your giving another percent without a qualm; when a friend you don't know well confides confused pain, and before you even think you say, "I'll pray for you," and you mean it and you do it believing your prayers will make a difference. That's Jesus coming to you in the Holy Spirit.

You, then, have the same experience as did those early Christians in Jerusalem when Jesus ascends, because he's gone only from sight. He reaches you now in ways you can understand because he's ascended not just into heaven, but into your very life. He's here again to bless you from the inside out with the kind of life he lived. As you follow Jesus you are amazed how often you now say, "Bye-bye" to things you thought you'd never part from without a great deal of suffering.

Communion

Our Lord Jesus is present and active still, raising us up to God's kind of heavenly life on earth. Let us trust the new and mysterious life he offers us as we share the feast at the table he has prepared. Amen.

---

1. Lori Wiener in Joanna Laufer and Kenneth Lewis, *Inspired Lives: Exploring the Role of Faith and Spirituality in the Lives of Extraordinary People* (Woodstock, Vermont: Skylight Paths Publishing, 1998), pp. 19-20.

Jesus' Prayer: The Pause in the Battle

In 1936, near the beginning of the Spanish Civil War one horrible center of fighting was the Alcázar fortress near Toledo. In the middle of horrific fighting, however, every day the firing stopped twice in order to allow a blind beggar to tap his way on the street between the firing lines. We can imagine how welcome those few minutes were to the men on both sides. They probably hoped that the blind man walked slower to give them a few more seconds of peace. Then the reprieve ended and the slaughter again engulfed the two armies that were struggling to kill each other.[1]

We meet Jesus in a similar critical moment. He's in the middle of a few hours of relief between his antagonists' struggling to arrest him and their final success—apprehending him at night and dragging him to trial and death. So, today's text is the pause in John's gospel just before Jesus' arrest, trial, and crucifixion. Immediately before our text in chapter 13, Jesus shares his last meal with his students, washing their feet and teaching them from his humble example. Then in chapters 14 to 16 he continues teaching. Finally, in chapter 17 he offers his prayer in his last few minutes of peace. This break in the fury ends soon. Under cover of darkness the soldiers and police arrest him on the Mount of Olives. From there the action continues downward to his destruction.

In this short interval before he's whisked off to suffer and die, Jesus prays at the end of his public influence. All we need do is remember that our prayers get more honest the closer we come to danger, and we'll understand how to evaluate Jesus' prayer. He prays here for what he most cares about. In his prayer we listen to the rock bottom of his concerns.

I heard of an agnostic who was very interested in peace and justice. One day, hoping that the Christian church would have something to say about achieving a world of peace and justice, he attended worship. It was a congregation, however, whose manner of prayer was to say "just" in every sentence. He reported, "They prayed, 'O Lord just help us… just give us… just protect us… just be merciful to us.' I realized that instead of 'justice' all they cared about was 'just us.' " In this portion of his prayer Jesus prays just for his students; but, beyond where we read today he expands his prayer to include all who will believe because of them. That's a huge prayer for Jesus and a big assignment for us. Our faith isn't merely about us but about our reaching others with Jesus' faith, compassion, and healing.

As we live for Jesus our lives aren't perfect. As we pray, our prayers aren't perfect and others can misunderstand our prayers. If the truth be told, on the scale of what's necessary we often, even in our religious life, focus on what ranks second or third (or twenty-eighth or twenty-ninth). Our life with God can be like a cross-country race between four runners. The first runner is splendid and soon is so far ahead that he's out of sight. One runner is slow and soon lags way behind. The only race interesting for its competition is between two equally able runners. Pretty soon everyone at the meet is watching those two battle for second and third and almost forget who's the best in the whole race. The church can be like that as we major in minors. We settle for the pretty good instead of the best. Jesus' prayer faces us with what is and who is supremely important.

In the little time left in Jesus' earthly life he doesn't teach us directly any longer. He lets us listen in as he prays and allows us to be affected by it. Shakespeare's contemporary Ben Johnson said, "Language most shows the man: speak that I may see thee." When Jesus speaks to God, we perceive who he really is. We see his self-understanding and his intensions. We view his determination and his pain.

He's about to die; yet he prays for us. If I were about to die, I'd be praying for me. Jesus prays for us. We've all known that people pray for us. Sometimes, although those prayers for us certainly reach God, they haven't affected us. Maybe in the past prayers for us have seemed to bounce off our soul like a fire hose only splattering water against a brick wall. Or we've actively defended ourselves from prayers, batting them away like playing tennis. Sometimes it's a while before even Jesus' prayers truly get through to us.

The seventeenth-century scientist and philosopher Blaise Pascal still amazes those who study him. He had mastered Latin and Greek by the time he was twelve. He devised a way to measure an angled cross-section of a cone, invented the world's first calculating machine, investigated the dynamics of liquids, experimented with the barometer, and developed a theory of probability before dying at 39. Historians approach Pascal from different perspectives, but they all rate him a genius.

Humans can use our intelligence to hold God at arm's length. Pascal had believed in God but wandered away from his devotion until he drifted into despair. Then one night as he faced God he read this prayer of Jesus in John 17, and he seemed surrounded by God's fire of love. He experienced the highest and grandest of ecstasy in God's presence for two hours. His life was totally changed there within God's presence and Jesus' prayer for him. He redirected his genius toward defending the Christian faith and commending to others Jesus as the very character of God on earth.

As with Blaise Pascal, Jesus' prayer and God's presence don't meet on the page of the Bible. They join in our lives now. When our youngest daughter was in college I was surfing the channels one night, and I came across her college basketball team on TV. I watched and, as the camera panned over the fans, I peered into the stands, and there's Lydia, jumping, waving, and yelling her throat out. I knew she always had her cell phone with her. So I phoned and when she answered I said, "Hey Lyd, I just saw you on TV at the basketball game."

She said, "No you didn't."

"Yes I did. I'm positive I saw you screaming like a fiend. You're in the stands in the gym."

"No, I'm not."

I was confused. "I'm sure that you —"

She said, "The game was last night. It's a rebroadcast."

When you read Jesus' prayer, it's not history. It's not even a believable rebroadcast. Jesus prays for us right now. He prays, "*Now* they know that everything you have given me is from you" (v. 7). If we don't have any access to the living God now, if we have no sense or experience of God now, why study the Bible about Jesus way back then? Our experience with Jesus — like that of Blaise Pascal — can be that of God's fiery presence right now. Or our life with Jesus can be like that daily pause in the Spanish Civil War in 1936 — that necessary time and space needed for bare survival. Our meeting Jesus in his prayer is more than a chance to gasp in the middle of a too fast, too confusing, or too dangerous life. Jesus, in prayer, offers to give us a whole new pattern for living.

E.L. Doctorow set his novel of the American Civil War in General Sherman's "march to the sea." It's titled *The March*. In it Doctorow portrays in fictional form not only real things that happened in the Civil War, but things that happen in our lives. The Union forces set fire to the cotton in Columbia, South Carolina, and the sparks from the cotton spread and begin to ignite the city. The flames leap from one neighborhood to the next block and now a convent school is in danger of burning. The Abbess Sister Ann Marie comes leading the 25-30 children out of the fire. The Union soldiers posted to guard them have no choice but to follow. She commands the children not to cry, to look only at the ground as they walk, and to trust God to protect them. They follow her out through the danger, and right there is a tiny spot of order in the center of chaos, a group of believers walking by faith if not by sight.[2]

That's much the way Jesus leads us in this world, even if all we see is the back of his legs in the smoke. No matter what we have to go through, he says, "Follow me." Our faith in Jesus grants us new and certain direction when all around us is falling apart. Jesus even leads us toward a world of peace and justice, teaching us to love our enemies and pray for those who persecute us. The best way for us to appropriate such a gigantic life-change is to pray.

Jesus, while he's in danger, prays for his students. Not only will he be arraigned, found guilty, and executed, but in his trial Jesus will be questioned about his students. Jesus prayed for his students before they too were in danger. He prays for us before we're in danger, and God's presence answers Jesus' prayer for us right now — sometimes with holy fire surrounding us but always with a leader who guides us through everything, even a world that's burning down around us.

Here, this moment, in whatever circumstances we suffer, in whatever dangers that ambush us from the outside or surprise us from the inside, now, no matter what race we're in and seem to be losing or what manner of civil war rages inside of us demanding that we give our attention, energy and loyalty to something that is less than eternal, now — when we really need it — Jesus prays for us.

We can become distracted by things around us: the rising price of gas or the falling value of houses. We can be preoccupied by the things about us: losing our youth or losing our faculties, losing our confidence or losing our reputation.

We're well advised in all situations to concentrate upon what Jesus prays for us. He prays that God protect us in God's name.

Our culture has slowly changed how a person is named. Nowadays many parents make up a name for their child that no one else has used. Even former generations gave names that only vaguely generated sentiment by granting a child the name of a forebear or of a favorite friend. So it's hard for us from our culture and experience to understand the significance of names in the Bible. In the biblical world names often expressed something about the person or at least carried the parents' hope for their child. Names in the Bible were like names among Shoshoni warriors in the 17 and 1800s. They had meaning, and they changed. So, doing historical research about Shoshoni warriors is confusing. At different times in their lives they'd receive a different name because they'd fought well in battle or perhaps stole a good herd of horses. The name changed because it announced something of the man's character or achievement.[3]

Jesus demonstrates God's character and power (meaning God's name) when, instead of praying for himself, he prays for those he loves. Thus, he reveals God's true nature. And Jesus does it now. As we read the Bible and hear Jesus' prayer, it's not a rebroadcast or a rerun. It's not the repetition of someone else's experience or even a memory of our own past relationship with God. It's meeting God right here in the gauntlet we walk through life, now when we are desperate for faith but frightened to lose control of ourselves, here where conflicts rage within us and we long for that gentle pause that God provides those who entrust themselves to Jesus.

We'll never get all we want from God in this life. Jesus, however, makes sure we get all we need. He protects us in God's name, the name Jesus prays in verse 11 *that God has given to him.* Jesus bears God's name. We realize that God's name, God's personality, God's character and deepest nature are most clearly seen in the one who prays for us and in whose name we pray: Jesus.

Let us pray, Lord Jesus, thank you that you've reached into our lives with your compassion. We praise you that, for no merit of our own, you love us, forgive us, and invite us to follow you through life and eternity. Lord, help us to spread your word to others, to pray for others as you have prayed for us, and to give our lives in your service to others. We'll try to concentrate only on you, no matter our problems. We'll try merely to look at your heels as we follow you through life's fires and trust that, when the flames are highest and hottest, they also can carry within them the very presence of God. As you prayed to the heavenly Father, so do we, offering our prayer in your name. Amen.

Communion

Let us follow our Lord Jesus to his table. Here Jesus' words and actions combine with the Holy Spirit to reach us now with the very presence of God. Amen.

---

1. Antony Beevor, *The Battle for Spain: The Spanish Civil War 1936-1939* (London: Penguin, 2006), p. 122.
2. E.L. Doctorow, *The March* (New York: Random House, 2005), pp. 178-179.
3. Gale Ontko, *Thunder over the Ochoco: The Gathering Storm, Volume 1* (Bend, Oregon: Maverick, 1993), p. xvi.